A-L[STUDENT GUIDE

AQA

Sociology

Topics in sociology (Families and households and Beliefs in society)

Joan Garrod and Laura Pountney

HODDER
EDUCATION
AN HACHETTE UK COMPANY

This Guide has been written specifically to support students preparing for the AQA A-level Sociology examinations. The content has been neither approved nor endorsed by AQA and remains the sole responsibility of the author.

Every effort has been made to trace all copyright holders, but if any have been inadvertently overlooked, the Publishers will be pleased to make the necessary arrangements at the first opportunity.

Although every effort has been made to ensure that website addresses are correct at time of going to press, Hodder Education cannot be held responsible for the content of any website mentioned in this book. It is sometimes possible to find a relocated web page by typing in the address of the home page for a website in the URL window of your browser.

Hachette UK's policy is to use papers that are natural, renewable and recyclable products and made from wood grown in well-managed forests and other controlled sources. The logging and manufacturing processes are expected to conform to the environmental regulations of the country of origin.

Orders: please contact Bookpoint Ltd, 130 Park Drive, Milton Park, Abingdon, Oxon OX14 4SE. Telephone: (44) 01235 827827. Fax: (44) 01235 400401. Email: education@bookpoint. co.uk. Lines are open from 9 a.m. to 5 p.m., Monday to Saturday, with a 24-hour message answering service. You can also order through our website: www.hoddereducation.co.uk.

© Joan Garrod and Laura Pountney 2020

ISBN 978-1-5104-7203-7

First printed 2020

First published in 2020 by
Hodder Education,
An Hachette UK Company
Carmelite House
50 Victoria Embankment
London EC4Y 0DZ

www.hoddereducation.co.uk

Impression number 10 9 8 7 6 5 4 3 2 1

Year 2024 2023 2022 2021 2020

Cover photo: Dmytro/stock.adobe.com

Typeset by Integra Software Services Pvt. Ltd, Pondicherry, India

Printed in Dubai

A catalogue record for this title is available from the British Library

Contents

Content Guidance

Questions & Answers

■ Getting the most from this book

Exam tips

Advice on key points in the text to help you learn and recall content, avoid pitfalls, and polish your exam technique in order to boost your grade.

Knowledge check

Rapid-fire questions throughout the Content Guidance section to check your understanding.

Knowledge check answers

1 Turn to the back of the book for the Knowledge check answers.

Summaries

■ Each core topic is rounded off by a bullet-list summary for quick-check reference of what you need to know.

Exam-style questions

Commentary on the questions

Tips on what you need to do to gain full marks.

Sample student answers

Practise the questions, then look at the student answers that follow.

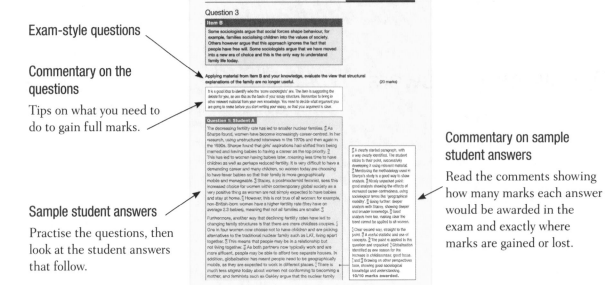

Commentary on sample student answers

Read the comments showing how many marks each answer would be awarded in the exam and exactly where marks are gained or lost.

◼ About this book

This guide covers the topics of *Families and households* and *Beliefs in society* in the AQA A-level specification 7192. The content reflects the linear structure of the course, where students have spent 2 years developing their sociological knowledge. The guide indicates and briefly explains and discusses those things that you should know and understand about these topics, but is intended to complement, not replace, your textbooks and class notes.

This guide is designed to help prepare students to answer all question types on Paper 2, Topics in Sociology. The question structures for the two topics are identical. This student guide provides examples of all questions for both topics.

How to use the book

The first main section of the book is **Content Guidance**. It follows the sequence of topics as they occur in the AQA specification, but it is not necessary to read them in this order, provided you make sure that you cover them all.

In your study of these topic areas you should examine the two **core themes**. These are:

■ socialisation, culture and identity
■ social differentiation, power and stratification

These are not things to be studied separately — rather, in your study of *Families and households* and *Beliefs in society* you should be aware of the two core themes running through the topics.

You should also be aware of both the **evidence** for and the **sociological explanations** of the content of these topics. This means that you must study the relevant sociological theories, perspectives and methods associated with these topics, as well as the design of the research used to obtain any data under consideration, including its strengths and limitations. The specification states that you should be involved with the research process and you should experience your own small-scale research, which you can mention in your answers where appropriate. In addition, you should be aware of the importance of conflict and consensus theories, social structure and social action, and the role of values.

Each section of the Content Guidance contains exam tips, knowledge checks and definitions of some key terms. Knowing and understanding the meaning of sociological concepts is an essential part of the whole course.

The second main section of the book contains **Questions & Answers**. At the beginning of this section are the three assessment objectives against which your exam answers will be judged, with some guidance regarding how to display the required skills, and also a list of command words, with explanations. The questions provided are in the style of the AQA exam for these topics, and are divided into questions for each topic. Each question has two student answers, one from a student whose answer is at the level of an A grade, and one from a student whose answer is at roughly a C grade.

Remember the importance of noting the structure and mark allocations of questions. Throughout the student answers, you will find comments, explaining why what has been written is good and is scoring well, and where things have gone wrong or there is room for improvement. More detailed guidance on how to use the Questions & Answers section is given at the beginning of that section.

Content Guidance

Families and households

■ The family, social structure and social change: the economy and social policies

All sociologists agree that the family is a very important part of the **social structure**, but there are disagreements about the role that the family plays for individuals and for society today. One function of the family is to prepare people for their role in the economy. Another function of the family is **socialisation**.

There are many aspects of family life that you may be asked about, including roles, structures and relationships. The economy, or the world of work, may well affect all three of these areas in different ways.

Structural and social action theories of the family

Structural theories claim that social forces shape people's position, roles and relationships in family life. These theories include functionalism, Marxism and feminism. Structural theories argue that the individual is passive and lacks free will or the ability to shape or negotiate their position in the family.

In contrast, social action theories claim that, rather than being shaped by social forces, people select or negotiate their own family experiences, roles and relationships. Therefore social action theories are different from structural theories as they argue that individuals have free will.

These two approaches are reflected in the way that family life is researched, with structural approaches taking a more macro, large-scale approach while social action thinkers argue that a smaller-scale or micro approach should be taken in order to understand the meanings attached to family life.

Modern and postmodern views of the family

Modern theories of the family include functionalism and Marxism, while feminism and social action theories are considered late modern (this also includes the sociology of personal life). Modern theorists make a number of assumptions about family life and society more generally which affect their views on the nature of family life. Modern social theorists usually agree that:

- the family is generally stable and often nuclear
- identity is generally fixed and predictable
- religion plays a role in shaping people's attitudes towards family life

Social structure The social institutions in a society (e.g. the education system, religious organisations) and also the patterns of social relationships between people and groups (e.g. the class structure, kinship networks).

Socialisation The internalisation of norms and values, with primary socialisation taking place before a child starts school and secondary socialisation taking place throughout life.

- family life can be understood through structural forces (functionalists, Marxists and feminists) or through meanings (social action theorists)
- people are likely to conform in part to what is expected as a social norm, in terms of expectations regarding family life

However, other sociologists believe that contemporary society is now in a postmodern stage, where these assumptions are no longer useful. Postmodern theorists argue that in order to understand family life in a globalised world, alternative theoretical ideas are necessary. Postmodern sociologists argue that family life today is generally characterised by the following:

- more fluid and complex identities
- the availability of an increasing range of choices in relation to family roles, relationships and structures
- a greater variety of family structures and forms emerging as a result of more rapid globalisation (increasing interconnectedness)
- a tendency for people to be more individualistic, placing their own needs and wishes above what is expected by others, so that individuals are less likely to conform to particular traditional ideas

Functionalist views of the family

Functionalists take a structural view, which means that they believe social forces shape human behaviour. They argue that institutions such as the family work together in a similar way to organs working together in the body, which they call an organic analogy. Functionalists claim that the family benefits the individual and society. They accept that at times the family is dysfunctional, or fails to function, but they see this as being rare.

George Murdock

In 1949 the functionalist George Murdock published research from his study of a sample of 250 societies, from less developed and developed countries, including America. He concluded that even though there were variations, the 'nuclear family' was universal. The nuclear family was characterised by:

- common residence
- economic cooperation
- reproduction

Murdock also believed that the nuclear family performed four basic functions for society. These were sexual, reproductive, economic and educational, with the educational function including socialisation within the family.

Talcott Parsons

The American sociologist Talcott Parsons, writing in the 1950s, claimed that the nuclear family had become more specialised and had shed some of its earlier functions, which were now taken over or shared by other bodies in society, such as the education system. Parsons argued that modern nuclear families performed two essential functions for society. The first was the primary socialisation of children. The second was the stabilisation of the adult personality — this meant that families

Knowledge check 1

If primary socialisation takes place largely within the family, where does secondary socialisation take place?

provided a safe haven for adults, helping them to cope with the stresses and strains of modern living.

Parsons was interested in how tasks were divided between male and female partners, also known as the division of labour. He believed that the male and female should play what he saw as their 'natural' roles, which complemented each other and ensured stability in society. The male role was the **instrumental role**, by which he meant being the breadwinner. The female role was the **expressive role**, caring for and nurturing the children and looking after the home.

Knowledge check 2

To what extent do you think there is evidence to support the idea that the instrumental and expressive roles for males and females are 'natural'?

Exam tip

It is important to acknowledge that many functionalist ideas are now considered less relevant to society today. There have been many significant social changes since functionalists developed their ideas.

Evaluation

- + Draws attention to the importance of the family as an institution in society.
- + Shows how the family links to the economy.
- + Shows the positive side of family life for individuals and for society.
- – Fails to recognise alternative family forms — the nuclear family is no longer the dominant family structure.
- – Model based on traditional white middle-class family.
- – Sees the division of labour between the sexes as 'natural' rather than learned behaviour.
- – Ignores negative effects of the family such as domestic violence, subordination of women.

New Right views of the family

New Right views are primarily political, rather than sociological, and have had a significant influence on British social policies on the family introduced under Conservative and coalition governments.

Charles Murray

Like other New Right thinkers, Murray (1984) is concerned with what he sees as the negative effects caused to individuals and to society by the breakdown of the so-called traditional nuclear family. This breakdown is evidenced by issues such as the rising rates of cohabitation, divorce and single parenthood, and the growth of a **culture of dependency** which is passed down through the generations. Murray believes that too-generous welfare benefits are largely to blame for many of society's ills.

The New Right believe that individuals should take responsibility for themselves, with the minimum of state intervention. Murray is known for his development of the concept of 'the underclass', a group characterised by what he saw as deviant attitudes towards parenting, work and crime. New Right ideas can be seen in the policies of the Conservative government from 2010, with the shrinking role of the state and reductions in welfare benefits.

Culture of dependency An alleged set of values brought about by over-generous welfare benefits, leading recipients to rely on 'handouts' from the state rather than finding work and providing for themselves and their children.

Evaluation

- + Draws attention to some of the negative effects of family breakdown for individuals and society.
- – Sees all changes to the traditional nuclear family as negative.
- – Fails to recognise other factors that can cause family problems and breakdown, such as domestic violence, unemployment, low wages, poor housing, racism.
- – No evidence for existence of 'underclass'.

Marxist views of the family

Marxists take a structural view and claim that the family plays an important part in maintaining the capitalist system, a system based on pursuing profit and private ownership of property.

Friedrich Engels

Engels (1884) believed that family structure evolved over time, and the monogamous nuclear family developed with the emergence of a class society based on private property. Engels argued that the wealthy wanted to make sure they passed down their money to the next generation and therefore the idea of a **monogamous nuclear family** emerged, with a male head and a female wife who would bear only his children and who also provided the emotional support.

Eli Zaretsky

Zaretsky, in his book *Capitalism, the Family and Personal Life* (1976), focused on the family as a refuge for individuals, particularly workers, from the alienation caused by capitalism. His argument was that as it provided much-needed relief and comfort to people, the nuclear family acted as a major prop to capitalism. In other words, the family performed an 'ideological function'. The family also served capitalism in other ways: through the (unpaid) domestic work of women, through the reproduction of the labour force and as an important unit of consumption.

Louis Althusser

Althusser (1971) saw the family as one of the ideological state apparatuses, that is, those institutions that served capitalism by socialising people into accepting that capitalism and an unequal class society were 'normal' — for example, by teaching children to accept authority.

Evaluation

- + Shows a link between family structure and the economy.
- + Takes a critical look at the family.
- + Shows how the family is part of the ideological state apparatus.
- – Links everything about the family to the capitalist economic structure — economic determinism.
- – Ignores other reasons for marriage, such as romantic love.
- – Focuses on the negative aspects of the family.
- – By focusing only on capitalism, ignores other forms of oppression, e.g. patriarchy.

Monogamous nuclear family In Engels' view, a family type which supports the emergence of capitalism: a heterosexual married couple, with children who inherit wealth from their parents.

Knowledge check 3

What is meant by monogamy?

Feminist views of the family

There are various feminist views of the family, but most of them take a highly critical look at how the family affects women. They argue that the family is patriarchal, or male-dominated.

Marxist feminists

Marxist feminists view women as being dually exploited by the family and by capitalism: as well as carrying out unpaid housework, women are expected to absorb men's frustration with capitalism and raise children to accept capitalist ideology.

Radical feminists

Radical feminists see relationships in the family as damaging for women and believe that huge changes are necessary to overcome **patriarchy**. They believe that women are oppressed and experience domestic violence, control by men and a lack of power in the family.

> **Patriarchy** Male-dominated society, or a set of ideas which support the idea that men are more powerful than women.

Liberal feminists

Liberal feminists are optimistic about women's position within the family, due to changes in attitudes and laws which have led to greater equality. They believe, however, that women are still often expected to do many mundane and repetitive jobs while working in paid employment at the same time.

Difference feminists

Difference feminists believe that women's experience of patriarchy varies from woman to woman and cannot be generalised to 'all women'. They believe that much has to be done to address the current position of women in the family, exploring differences in class, ethnicity and location. Difference feminists can also argue that men and women are inherently different, and that we should accept this difference and try to understand it rather than attempting to maintain equality.

Evaluation

- ■ + Challenges the traditional view that gendered roles are 'natural'.
- ■ + Focuses on patriarchy as inbuilt into society's institutions, including the family.
- ■ + Shows the negative side of family life, especially for women.
- ■ − Some views fail to recognise the diversity of family life.
- ■ − Tends to assume that all women are oppressed within the family, and ignores the positive aspects of family life for women.

Social action theories of the family

Another approach comes from social action theories of the family, sometimes known as interpretivist theories of the family. This approach claims that rather than family life being shaped by structural forces, as functionalists, Marxists and feminists claim, in fact individuals have agency and can negotiate their position in the family.

This approach argues that it is important to take a micro or small-scale approach in order to understand the meanings that people attach to family life. For example, by exploring marriage on the small scale, the interpretivist Clarke (1991) argues that there is not one type of marriage but many types, all of which take on different meanings and are negotiated by the individuals involved.

Unlike postmodernists, who claim we act in terms of our own individual needs and wishes (individualism), social action theorists argue that people today are still very much part of sets of important relationships.

The sociology of personal life

One branch of social action theory that has recently emerged is known as 'the sociology of personal life'. This approach argues that to understand family life it is necessary to explore the meanings people attach to relationships within and beyond the family, including for example pets and **fictive kin**, or people who are regarded as family but who may not be formally part of family life. Carole Smart (2007) argues that it is better to use the words 'personal life' rather than 'families' to describe relationships today because we can no longer assume that people choose traditional family models. Rather, Smart argues that people choose to negotiate their own particular forms of relationships.

Fictive kin People who are seen as part of the family but who are not related by blood, birth or marriage.

This approach involves new methods of understanding family life, for example through looking at the particular memories people have of family events and what they choose to remember, and exploring changes to relationships over time rather than just looking at family structures. Nordqvist and Smart (2014) argue that biology and marriage-based relationships are less significant today than they have been in the past, so this approach is useful since it acknowledges the importance of other significant relationships in people's lives.

Postmodern views of the family

Postmodern views, which developed more recently from the 1980s onwards, believe that the 'metanarrative' or grand, overarching explanations of the modern period, such as Marxism and science, are no longer sufficient to explain and make sense of contemporary family life. Rather, they see postmodern families as characterised by fragmentation, diversity, individualism and choice.

There is no longer any single ideal family type. Individuals decide for themselves whether they wish to marry, cohabit or remain alone, whether to have children or not, and what kind of relationship(s) they wish to have. Evidence of this is the increasing diversity of family and household structures found in Western societies.

Ulrich Beck

Beck (1992) saw the family in postmodern society as being characterised by 'risk', meaning that there was a much higher chance of divorce and other types of family breakdown and instability.

Judith Stacey

Stacey (1996), a postmodernist feminist, carried out research into family life in Silicon Valley, California, in the USA. She found that women in particular benefit from the increased choice that people have today about how to organise family life and what sorts of relationships to have in a global postmodern society. She claims that women have not been in a position to enjoy such choices until now.

Evaluation

- ■ + Draws attention to diversity of family structures.
- ■ + Links changes in families to wider changes such as globalisation and fragmentation of class structure.
- ■ − Overemphasises the degree of choice in people's lives, particularly for some women.
- ■ − Ignores the fact that most family patterns remain fairly traditional or close to this structure.

Knowledge check 4

What is meant by a metanarrative?

The changing family and the economy

Some sociologists, such as Talcott Parsons, have linked the nuclear family structure to industrial society. The suggestion was that in preindustrial societies the extended family was the dominant structure, but that with urbanisation and the growth of industry, the nuclear family became the norm. This is because before industrialisation, the family was a unit of production, making goods together to sell, whereas in industrial society, the family becomes a unit of consumption, earning a wage and buying goods and services. Parsons calls this process the 'theory of fit'. The family, therefore, responds to changes in society by making particular adaptations to make it 'fit' better.

Peter Willmott and Michael Young

Two other writers who saw a link between family structure and composition and the economic structure were Willmott and Young (1974). They saw the family in industrial society as symmetrical — the welfare state had taken over many of the functions previously performed by families. The family consisted of a married couple whose roles mirrored each other, sharing household responsibilities as well as paid work.

Evaluation

- ■ + Important to look at the relationship between the family and other institutions in society, particularly the economy.
- ■ − Fails to recognise the importance of class to family and household structure.
- ■ − The 'fit thesis' is not borne out by evidence; many suggest that there has always been family diversity.

The family and social policies

It is important to remember that social policies transmit ideas and values. Social policies on the family may both respond to social problems (such as a high divorce rate) and offer a model of what those in power think families *ought* to be like.

Right-wing views on the family

Right-wing ideology tends to be associated with the New Right and (in Britain) with the Conservative Party, who believe that the state, or government, should play a smaller role in family life. They argue that the individual should take responsibility for their family. Since coming into office in 2010, the Conservative Party has made significant cuts to welfare spending on supporting poorer families. They believe that the nuclear family is the ideal family structure.

Examples of recent right-wing social policies include the following:

■ Private ownership of housing in response to the housing crisis — the government aim to build 300,000 homes a year by the mid-2020s (2019).
■ The reintroduction of married persons' tax allowance (2015).
■ The Welfare Reform Act (2012) — this introduced universal credits, a replacement welfare support policy with much stricter application criteria and a stronger emphasis on getting people back to work.
■ Substantial cuts to the Legal Aid budget (2013), meaning less free legal advice for vulnerable groups such as women in abusive relationships.
■ Troubled Families (2011) — a policy designed to tackle families with significant problems such as dependency issues, worklessness and crime.

Left-wing views on the family

Left-wing ideology tends to be associated with the Labour Party, who believe that the state, or government, should play an important role in family life. They argue that although the nuclear family is ideal, alternatives to it should be supported and valued.

Examples of left-wing policies between 1997 and 2010 include the following:

■ Paternity Rights (2003) — this extended maternity rights to fathers, including two weeks of unpaid leave.
■ The New Deal (1998) — this helped lone parents to re-enter employment by assisting with childcare and education costs.
■ The Adoption and Children Act (2002) — this act allowed same-sex couples to adopt. It also ensured that the views and wishes of children were heard.
■ The Civil Partnership Act (2004) — this allowed same-sex couples to be publicly and legally recognised as being partners.

There are different theoretical perspectives on social policies and the family, as outlined below.

The functionalist view

Functionalists see a stable family as very important for society. The 'march of progress' theory sees developments in education, health and working practices as helping families to fulfil their important functions of the appropriate socialisation of children and providing a safe and stable environment for adults.

Exam tip

Remember that you may be asked about the effects of social policies on family structures, roles or relationships. You may also be asked about the effects of social policy on the experience of childhood.

Exam tip

Remember that, although some policies from the left and right reflect the different views of the respective governments, there are some policies which reflect changes in society more generally, such as equality legislation.

The Marxist view

Marxists view all state social policies as designed to serve the interests of capitalism. Therefore family policies — such as supporting parents or making it easier for women to join the labour force — are all designed to ensure that capitalism has the workforce that it needs. Policies promoting 'family values' such as obedience and respect for authority are designed to ensure an obedient and compliant future workforce.

The New Right view

New Right thinkers do not approve of too much state intervention in people's lives, including the family. They are against what they see as too-generous benefits to 'deviant' households such as those with lone parents and non-working households. Their argument is that such benefits lead to a 'culture of dependency', which makes people over-reliant on the state and robs them of the incentive to find work. There is evidence of these views in the Conservative government which since 2010 has been shrinking the role of the state in family life to save money, under an 'austerity' programme.

The feminist view

Feminists are against policies which they see as upholding patriarchy, such as different entitlements for female and male employees following the birth of a child (note that there are now new policies on this), policies that penalise lone parents, most of whom are women, and policies that reflect the view that mothers are primarily responsible for their children's behaviour. They support policies that benefit women, such as those allowing abortion, making divorce easier, punishing domestic violence and giving legal rights to same-sex partnerships. Feminists are highly critical of recent New Right policies which have reduced welfare spending, known as 'austerity' policies, since they particularly affect women, who already tend to be poorer.

Evaluation

- + Sociologists highlight how reductions in state spending have increased inequalities in society, for example significant levels of child poverty.
- – Some policies seem to be strongly focused on the traditional nuclear family, to the detriment of other types of family structure.

Key concepts

social structure; primary socialisation; nuclear family; extended family; domestic division of labour; underclass; capitalism; ideological state apparatus; patriarchy; industrialisation

> **Exam tip**
>
> Remember that you may be asked how useful a particular theory is in understanding family life in contemporary society. Think about which theory you believe is most useful and why.

> **Knowledge check 5**
>
> What is the role of the state according to New Right thinkers?

> **Exam tip**
>
> Remember that there is no single 'feminist view', although there are some shared beliefs. Showing your knowledge of different types of feminism could gain you additional marks.

> **Knowledge check 6**
>
> What is the difference between radical and liberal feminist views on social policy for the family?

Summary

- All sociologists agree that the family plays an important role in society.
- There are consensus and conflict theoretical ideas about the exact relationship between the family and the wider social structure.
- Changes in the family both lead to and reflect changes in the wider social structure.
- The family remains an important focus of social policy, though sociologists disagree about the purpose, desirability and effects of different social policies.

Family diversity, changing patterns of relationships, childbearing and the life course

While the following summarises the main changes, you should be aware that there are differences, often significant ones, between groups based on social class, ethnic group, religion, age and sexual orientation.

Marriage

Britain is a monogamous society, in which people legally can have only one spouse at a time. In all societies, marriage is regulated in some way, with laws or norms governing who may marry whom. According to the Office for National Statistics (ONS):

- In 2016, there were 249,793 marriages in England and Wales.
- Of all marriages, 97.2% were between opposite-sex couples and 2.8% were between same-sex couples.
- There were 7,019 marriages between same-sex couples in 2016, an increase of 8.1% from 2015; of these marriages, 55.7% were between female couples.
- For the first time ever, less than one quarter (24%) of all marriages in 2016 were religious ceremonies.
- Marriages for those aged 65 and over went up by 46% in a decade, from 7,468 in 2004 to 10,937 in 2014.
- Marriage remains an important part of family life. According to the most recent census (2011), 65% of all families in the UK include married couples.
- The average (mean) age of heterosexual marriage has been rising. The average age for men marrying in 2015 was 37.5 years, while for women it was 35.1 years.
- Remarriage is increasingly likely, as people are more likely to be **serial monogamists**.
- A Forced Marriage Unit was created in 2013. In 2018, the Forced Marriage Unit (FMU) gave advice or support related to a possible forced marriage in 1,196 cases. Forced and child marriages in the UK often take place for religious and cultural reasons and are associated with members of some minority ethnic groups.

Cohabitation

Cohabitation refers to couples who live together without being married.

- According to ONS data, in 2017 there were 3.3 million families with cohabiting couples in the UK, with the figure having more than doubled from 1.5 million in 1996.
- While for some cohabitation may be a permanent state, for many it is a temporary stage. Almost nine out of ten couples who marry have lived together before marriage.

Exam tip

Be sure to pay careful attention to the wording of the question. If you are asked to discuss relationships, make sure that you include all forms of relationships, with partners, children and extended family members such as grandparents. Fictive kin are important too.

Serial monogamy

The practice of having one long-term faithful relationship after another, which is much more common today.

Exam tip

Remember that marriage remains popular today. Despite the UK having very high divorce rates, many people remarry, which suggests that people still see it as important.

- Cohabitation often occurs after a divorce or separation, which explains why more than four out of every ten cohabiting couples are over the age of 40.
- One of the reasons for the growth in cohabitation is likely to be the decline in the **stigma** of this arrangement, though the sheer number of couples cohabiting is also an important factor in its growing acceptability.

Separation and divorce

There are three possible endings to a relationship: bereavement, separation or divorce. Rather than looking at the *number* of divorces, it is more useful to look at the divorce *rate*, which is the number of divorces per 1,000 married people per year. As a general trend, the divorce rate has increased since the 1970s but is now beginning to decline a little.

The UK has one of the highest divorce rates in the world. There are a number of reasons for increasing divorce rates, including changes in the law.

Key changes in divorce laws are as follows:

- The Divorce Reform Act (1969) introduced 'irretrievable breakdown' as a reason for divorce, leading to a significant increase in the number of divorces. Before this act, there had to be a specific reason for divorce such as adultery.
- The Matrimonial and Family Proceedings Act (1984) allowed couples to divorce after only 1 year of marriage.
- The Family Law Act (1996) increased the minimum time of being married before divorcing to 18 months. This introduced time for reflection and consideration of children's views, in an attempt to reduce the number of divorces.
- In 2019, it was announced that legal changes would be made to marriage so that a 'no-fault divorce' would be introduced. This is so that during the divorce process, nobody has to be 'blamed' for behaviour leading to a divorce. The argument is that a blame culture leads to harm to the couple and in particular the children who may find divorce a damaging process if parents are negative towards each other during the process.

> **Exam tip**
>
> Be aware of specific divorce reform laws so that you can show how divorce has become easier.

The following points provide some data on divorce and separation:

- In 2017, there were 8.4 divorces of opposite-sex couples per 1,000 married men and women aged 16 years and over — the lowest divorce rate since 1973 and a 5.6% decrease from 2016 (ONS data).
- According to the ONS (2017), unreasonable behaviour was the most common reason for opposite-sex couples divorcing, with 52% of wives and 37% of husbands petitioning on these grounds. It was also the most common reason for same-sex couples divorcing, accounting for 83% of divorces among women and 73% among men.
- Couples may separate, either legally or informally, instead of, or prior to, divorcing. The 2011 census found that almost 4% of the married population were not living together as a married couple.

> **Exam tip**
>
> Show an awareness of the fact that civil partnerships and same-sex marriages reflect a major shift in attitudes towards same-sex relationships.

> **Knowledge check 7**
>
> What is the difference between a forced marriage and an arranged marriage?

Stigma Social disapproval.

> **Exam tip**
>
> Be aware that cohabitation can vary enormously: for example, it can be temporary or as a trial run for marriage or as an alternative to marriage, a long-term stable relationship.

What are the consequences of divorce?

There are a number of effects of divorce on family diversity, including a greater number of lone-parent and lone-person households, remarriages and stepfamilies. High divorce rates add further evidence that serial monogamy is becoming more common.

Remember, however, that the ending of relationships does not mean that parents stop parenting. Alternative arrangements to continue to parent children together, despite being separated, are more common, and are known as co-parenting arrangements. Children may also spend time with both parents if there is a divorce.

Childbearing and the life course

There have been some significant changes in the numbers of children born, which reflect wider changes in the roles of women and changing attitudes to family life.

- An important statistic when looking at childbearing is the total fertility rate (TFR). This is the average number of children born to a woman over her lifetime.
- After steadily falling from the high levels in Victorian times (apart from the 'baby booms' of the mid-1940s and 1960s), the 2011 census showed that the TFR for England and Wales had risen by 18% over the previous decade and stood at 1.9. The increase was put down largely to improvements in fertility treatment and the growing number of first-generation immigrant mothers, coming from societies where the norm for family size was higher than in the UK.
- In 2017, the total fertility rate (TFR) declined for the fifth consecutive year to 1.76 children per woman, from 1.81 in 2016.
- Fertility rates decreased for every age group in 2017, except for women aged 40 years and over. In that age group the rate increased by 1.3% to 16.1 births per 1,000 women, reaching the highest level since 1949.
- Fertility rates for non-British-born women are higher than those for British-born women: 28.4% of live births in 2017 were to mothers born outside the UK, following a gradual rise from 11.6% in 1990.

The following have been suggested as reasons for the fall in TFR since the 2011 census:

- changes to the benefits system
- uncertainty over employment in the economic recession
- the shortage of affordable housing
- the growing costs of raising a child

Another trend in childbearing is the rise in the average age of mothers giving birth. The average age of mothers giving birth in 2017 increased to 30.5 years, from 30.4 years in 2016 and 26.4 years in 1975.

Suggested reasons for this rise include:

- more women participating in higher education and going on to establish a career
- improvements in fertility treatment

Knowledge check 8

Give three reasons why the divorce rate has risen over the past 50 years.

Exam tip

The statistics are given to indicate the actual changes. You do not need to memorise them all in detail, but you should be able to discuss the trends that they represent, together with some suggested reasons for these.

According to statistics, in 2018 teenage pregnancy rates in the UK had halved since 2010, but rates of teenage pregnancy remain among the highest in Europe. Suggested reasons for the recent decrease include:

- programmes of sex and relationship education in schools
- targeted support for those deemed most at risk
- rising aspirations among many teenage girls

Life course analysis

Over the course of a person's life, they are likely to be part of different households and to play different roles. Some sociologists now argue that rather than discuss 'the family', we should discuss the family over a period of time, to understand people's decisions about family structure, roles and relationships and to explore the meanings behind these stages. Given that people are now living longer, they are also more likely to find themselves moving through a wider range of family arrangements. This approach is similar to the sociology of personal life or the interactionists' social action theory.

Family and household structures

Contemporary Britain is characterised by a large variety of **family** types and **household** structures. Class, ethnicity and age all exert an influence and result in differences between groups, but there are some visible trends over the population as a whole. Remember that people are not in fixed household structures — in fact, family structures change over time, and as people live for longer, they may pass through a range of family and household structures over time.

Much of the information about family and household types comes from the census, the latest of which was in 2011, which also allows comparison with data from earlier censuses.

What are the recent patterns?

- In 2017 there were 19.0 million families in the UK, a 15% increase from 16.6 million in 1996.
- With 12.9 million families, the married or civil partner couple family remained the most common type in 2017, with the cohabiting couple family growing the fastest.
- In the UK there were 27.2 million households in 2017, resulting in an average household size of 2.4.
- In 2017, there were 3.9 million people living alone aged 16 to 64 years, of which a larger proportion were male (58.5%). Similarly, there were 3.8 million people living alone aged 65 and over, but a larger proportion (66.5%) were female.
- Young males were more likely to be living with their parents than young females; in 2017, around 32% of males aged 20 to 34 years were living with their parents, compared with 20% of females aged 20 to 34 years.

'Living alone' does not necessarily mean not being in a relationship. Research has found that more than one in five people classified as single are actually in a relationship — this represents around 5 million people, or around 9% of adults in

Exam tip

Remember that there are differences among social and ethnic groups. Teenage births, for example, are more common among working-class than middle-class females, while older mothers are more likely to be found among the middle classes. Pointing out these differences shows good and accurate knowledge.

Family Defined by marriage, civil partnership or cohabitation or the presence of children in the household.

Household Defined as a person living alone or a group of people who live and eat at least one meal a day together.

Knowledge check 9

Give two reasons to explain the rise in single-person households among the 45–64 age group.

Britain. A term has been coined for such people: 'LATs', or 'living apart together'. The increase in LATs is partly explained by the fact that women no longer need to be living with a man in order to pay bills, have a mortgage and so on.

There has been a sharp rise in the number of young adults living at home with their parents. Some of these have left home but returned again, so this group is sometimes referred to as the 'boomerang generation'. A major reason for this is financial pressures which are caused by:

- the increasing difficulty for first-time buyers to obtain a mortgage
- rising rents, especially in towns and cities
- high unemployment among young people
- paying off student loans

Family types

Sociologists have identified a number of family types and it is important to know what these are.

Nuclear family

This is the basic family structure, consisting of two adults and their offspring. It is sometimes called the isolated nuclear family, referring to its self-contained status. Geographical mobility has led to many nuclear families living at a considerable distance from their wider kin.

Extended family

This is where the family has been extended beyond the nuclear family. This can be in the form of a vertically extended family, consisting of three or more generations living together or in close proximity, or a horizontally extended family, for example a household that includes two adult siblings and their families.

Reconstituted family

This refers to a family in which at least one of the adults has a child or children from a previous relationship living with them and their new partner. This type is also known as a stepfamily or a blended family.

Beanpole family

This concept refers to the pattern where, because of increased life expectancy, families now tend to exist over three or more generations, but with each generation having fewer children. Julia Brannen identified this family type, and argues that having fewer children in each generation can make childhood a more isolated and lonely experience for some children.

Living apart together (LAT)

As people are prioritising careers and adopting new forms of relationships, being in a relationship and not living together is becoming increasingly common. Duncan and Phillips (2013) argue that this LAT relationship is often a way of seeing whether a relationship can become more serious, and frequently develops into cohabitation or marriage.

> **Exam tip**
>
> Remember that people do not stay in a particular family type permanently — they move through different types throughout the life course.

Empty-nest family

This is where the adult offspring have left home. As noted earlier, the rise of the 'boomerang generation' means that many young adults now return to 'the nest'.

What are the different sociological views on family diversity?

There are some who claim that diversity is occurring and is a positive thing, while others see family diversity as a sign that the nuclear family is in decline.

- Radical feminists regard the traditional nuclear family as damaging or oppressive for women, and see alternatives as representing a more positive approach to family life where women are able to develop their own more equal or liberated positions.
- Gillian Dunne (1999) argues that lesbian couples as an alternative to traditional nuclear family structures are more equal since they lack the traditional ingrained gender roles or gender scripts that occur within heterosexual couples.
- Functionalists such as Chester (1985) argue that although many women work, families on the whole have retained nuclear family structures. In fact, demographic trends suggest that although there are higher rates of divorce, many people choose to remarry, so people still aspire to nuclear family structures.
- Chester calls the nuclear family where both parents work the 'neo-conventional nuclear family', stating that people still retain their positive view of this family type.
- On the other hand, Giddens (1992) claims that people are less concerned with fulfilling traditional family roles and structures and are instead increasingly concerned with emotionally fulfilling relationships, or 'pure relationships', and that therefore family diversity is a positive thing and occurring to a much larger extent than before.
- Rhona and Robert Rapoport (1982) believe that the rapid changes brought about by globalisation and postmodernity result in much greater family diversity. They claim that this diversity takes many different forms, including cultural, life stage, organisational, generational and social class diversity (CLOGS for short).

Evaluation

- + Draws attention to the significant number of changes that have occurred to family and household structures.
- + Recognises the wide variety of family and household types.
- + Shows that social, cultural and economic factors help to shape both family and household structures.
- + Shows that marriage remains an important institution.

Key concepts

monogamy; serial monogamy; cohabitation; civil partnerships; same-sex marriage; divorce; separation; total fertility rate; household; lone-parent family; reconstituted family

Exam tip

Remember that you may be asked about the extent to which the nuclear family is still the dominant family structure. Although there may be fewer nuclear families, people may still aspire to the nuclear family, for example by living in reconstituted families.

Exam tip

Remember that family structures also affect the nature of the roles and relationships that people have, as well as shaping the experience of childhood.

Summary

- Relationships are changing significantly, divorce has become more socially acceptable and alternatives to marriage have increased.
- Despite the rise in cohabitation and single-person households, marriage remains an important institution.
- The laws governing marriage have changed, allowing same-sex couples in England and Wales to marry.
- Most cohabiting couples go on to marry.
- The divorce rate has slowed down, but four out of ten couples now marrying are likely to divorce.
- The average age of mothers giving birth has risen, largely due to female career opportunities, female participation in higher education, improvements in fertility treatment and women embarking on new relationships following separation or divorce.
- There has been an increase in reconstituted families.
- A growing number of couples who are in a relationship choose not to live together.
- Globalisation has led to increasing communication and travel, which has led to increasing migration and more opportunities to maintain relationships within and beyond the family.

Gender roles, domestic labour and power relationships within the family today

Gender roles

Gender roles refer to the ways in which tasks and responsibilities are divided up between men and women in the family. This includes not just adults but children and elderly people as well as other members of the extended family.

There are many aspects of gender roles: domestic work, emotion work (caring for people), childcare responsibilities, controlling money, making decisions and so on. Power relations are also significant, in terms of who has most control in the family.

There are different perspectives on gender roles within the family.

Gender roles Reflect the dominant values in society regarding appropriate behaviour and attitudes for males and females.

Knowledge check 10

How could you argue that gender roles are socially constructed?

Functionalist views

Functionalists such as Parsons believed that gendered domestic roles were based on biological differences and therefore 'natural': males took the instrumental role and were primarily responsible for being the breadwinner, while females took the expressive and nurturing role and were best suited for domestic work and childcare.

Marxist views

Marxists see the family as a site of exploitation, of both males and females, but particularly of females, whose domestic and child-raising tasks are unpaid labour for the capitalist economy.

Feminist views

Feminists strongly challenge the functionalist view of gendered domestic roles as 'natural'. Oakley's work (1974) on housewives showed that they saw domestic work as dull, repetitive and monotonous, with low status and little job satisfaction. Oakley argued that whether they like it or not, women's domestic role places on them the burden of housework and childcare. When women do take paid work outside the home, they still assume the main responsibility for domestic and childcare tasks — the '**dual burden**'.

'March of progress' views

Some writers, such as Young and Willmott (1973), believed there was evidence that the 'symmetrical family' was emerging, where household tasks, while still often gendered in nature, were more equitably shared between men and women. It is also argued that the development of new technologies means that even if women are still taking the major share of the work, their tasks have become much easier and less time-consuming.

Domestic labour: the evidence

What are the patterns?

According to research by the Office for National Statistics (2016), women continue to do more housework than men. They found that:

- Women carry out an overall average of 60% more unpaid work than men. On average men do 16 hours a week of unpaid work (which includes cooking, transport, childcare, adult care, housework, laundry and volunteering), compared to the 26 hours a week of unpaid work done by women.
- With regard specifically to cooking, childcare and housework, women perform more than double the proportion of unpaid work of those kinds compared to men.

What is the evidence that relationships are becoming more egalitarian?

- Lyonette and Crompton (2015) find that men are contributing more to the domestic division of labour, mainly because of increased pressure on women who are at work.
- Man-Yee Kan and Laurie (2016) argue that there is considerable variation in the division of labour according to ethnicity. Mixed background women have the lowest share of housework (65%) while Pakistani women have the greatest share (83%).

What is the evidence that relationships remain unequal?

- Feminists such as Oakley point out that women continue to do much of the housework despite working outside the home, which continues to create a 'dual burden' for many women.
- Man-Yee Kan (2016) found that generally women continue to do much more housework than men, although women with degrees tend to do less housework than women without degrees — there is variation in the types of jobs women do and the amount of housework they do. Furthermore, Man-Yee Kan found that African Caribbean and Indian men are more likely to help more with housework than white men.

Dual burden This refers to the situation where women have the strain of doing both domestic work and paid work.

Exam tip

Remember to mention that both attitudes towards domestic labour and its practice may be affected by social class, ethnicity, religion and age.

Knowledge check 11

What is the 'march of progress' view on relationships?

- According to Norman and Watt (2017), women spend around twice as long on housework as men do. In the UK, men spend an average of 34 minutes on housework and cooking for every hour that women spend.
- Dunscombe and Marsden (1993) found that in terms of emotion work, such as taking care of ill children, resolving family conflict and listening to problems, women continue to take the majority of responsibility, often feeling 'emotionally deserted' by their husbands. This results in women feeling that they now have a triple shift of paid work, domestic work and emotion work.

The sandwich generation

A relatively new gender role that has emerged involves middle-aged women in their forties and fifties. They are sometimes referred to as the 'sandwich generation'. This is because they are often 'sandwiched' between looking after adolescent and even adult offspring (the 'boomerang generation' because they keep returning home) and the care of their ageing parent or parents. Additionally, many women in this age group are providing often unpaid childcare by looking after their grandchildren while the parents are working.

We can therefore conclude that although there have been changes in both attitude and practice with regard to the gendered division of labour, it remains true that women still undertake the major share of household and domestic tasks, even when in paid employment themselves.

Power relationships

Power relationships within the family generally refer to those between the adult partners and between parents and children. By 'power', sociologists are usually referring to the ability of someone to make another person do something, even against their will. While there are examples of the abuse of power within families, such as domestic violence and child abuse, it is more common to be referring to issues of decision making — who decides where the family will live, how their income is spent, how to bring up the children and so on.

Anthony Giddens (2013) has suggested the emergence of a new relationship ideal, which he calls 'the **pure relationship**'. This is based on equality and negotiation between the partners. He says that such relationships will last only as long as they continue to offer personal fulfilment to both partners.

Traditionally, with the pattern of male breadwinner and stay-at-home mother, the male was the main decision maker. This was because men were typically providing the main income, were in higher-status jobs and had higher educational attainment. The increasing participation of women in the labour market has in many cases redefined such power relationships, although feminists typically believe that the existence of patriarchy in society still confers greater power on the male.

Other evidence that power is not equally distributed in relationships

- Vogler and Pahl (2001) found that decision making remains dominated by men taking the more serious decisions, which they claimed is because men earn more money than women.
- Hardill (1997) found that although women are earning more, men continue to take important decisions, which is further evidence that power relationships remain unequal.

Exam tip

This is one area in which it is vital to show that you are aware of significant differences in power relationships within families based on social class, age and, very importantly, ethnicity, where different ethnic groups may have very different cultural ideas and traditions regarding the exercise of power within the family.

Pure relationship A relationship based on emotional fulfilment and negotiation between partners.

The abuse of power

In some families, the power of one person over other members of the family is highly abusive in nature. Domestic violence is a common example.

Domestic violence

The charity Women's Aid defines domestic abuse as an incident or pattern of incidents of controlling, coercive, threatening, degrading and violent behaviour, including sexual violence, in the majority of cases by a partner or ex-partner, but also by a family member or carer. It is very common. In the vast majority of cases it is experienced by women and is perpetrated by men.

- In 2018, according to the Office for National Statistics, on average two women were killed by their partner or ex-partner every week in England and Wales.
- On average the police in England and Wales receive over 100 calls relating to domestic abuse every hour.
- The Survey of England and Wales estimates that 1.2 million women experienced domestic abuse in the year ending March 2017 and 4.3 million women aged 16–59 have experienced domestic abuse since the age of 16 (ONS, 2018).

Evaluation

- – Functionalists see gendered roles within the family as positive and natural, ignoring the negative consequences for many women.
- – Both Marxists and feminists largely see women's roles within the family in a negative way, ignoring the fact that many women enjoy at least some parts of their domestic and childcare tasks.
- + Feminists have drawn attention to the importance of women's roles within the family, an area previously ignored by sociologists.
- + Families are recognised as sites of power, with often negative consequences for women and children.

Key concepts

gender roles; domestic division of labour; instrumental role; expressive role; power relations; symmetrical family; domestic violence

> **Knowledge check 12**
>
> How might the increasing participation of women in paid employment affect power relationships within the family?

> **Knowledge check 13**
>
> Identify two reasons why domestic violence is an under-reported crime.

> **Exam tip**
>
> Always show that you are aware where there are problems with research, for example with a smaller sample size meaning that the results cannot be generalised, but make sure that you link the point you are making to the specific question.

Summary

- There is still evidence to suggest that relationships continue to follow traditional patterns, despite many women now working.
- While there have been improvements in some areas of family life, women continue to be responsible for most domestic labour and emotional work while men tend to hold more power because they still tend to earn more.
- Marxists and feminists have drawn attention to the ways in which females are exploited within the family.
- Marxists believe women's exploitation stems largely from capitalism, while feminists see it as a result of patriarchy.
- The family is a site of power, which can be abusive in nature.

■ Childhood: changes in the status of children in the family and society

Childhood is a social construct — that is to say, it is not defined simply by biological age, but is determined by the cultural norms and values of a society. Therefore what we understand by childhood varies by time, by place and by society. In any society, there are often considerable differences in the experience of childhood, both within and between different social class and ethnic groups, and also between genders.

Different views of childhood

'March of progress' views

Those who believe that childhood has got better over time are often referred to as 'march of progress' theorists. Some of the main evidence and arguments they put forward for their views are as follows:

- There has been a significant fall in the **infant mortality rate**. In 2016 the infant mortality rate was 3.8, whereas just over 100 years earlier, in 1911, the rate was 130.
- Fewer children are being born and families are smaller, which means that there is more time and energy given to children. This suggests that we now live in a more child-centred society.
- Children now remain in compulsory education until 18, meaning that there is a longer period when they do not have adult responsibilities and are economically dependent on adults.
- Increasingly, legislation has prevented children from having to work at a young age and has protected young people when they are at work, for example in the hours they can legally work and in the kinds of work that they are allowed to do.
- Children now have a number of legal rights to afford them protection.
- Specialist children's services have been introduced to protect and foster children's health and wellbeing.
- Research has been carried out into how children's bodies and minds develop, so there is a wealth of information about issues such as diet and appropriate play and learning activities.
- There is a huge range of age-appropriate toys and literature available.

Philippe Ariès (1960)

Ariès claimed that the modern view of childhood did not emerge until the seventeenth century. He examined portraits of children in medieval society. He argued that children were seen as 'mini adults'. The work of Ariès has been criticised for relying only on images of children from wealthy families in portraits, which is not representative of all children of the time.

> **Exam tip**
>
> Make sure you understand why we know childhood is a social construct. Evidence comes from differences in the experience of childhood in different times in the past and in different places around the world.

> **Infant mortality rate**
> The number of deaths per year in the first year of life per 1,000 live births.

> **Exam tip**
>
> Make quite sure that you understand differences of wording in questions about childhood. If you are asked about the 'experience' of childhood, you are being asked if it is positive or negative. If you are asked about the 'changing status' of children, you are being asked if society has become more child-centred.

Conflict views

Others argue that childhood in Western societies, including the UK, has got worse over time. They can be described as holding conflict views of childhood. They offer the following as arguments and evidence:

- The number of children on child protection plans from 2014 to 2018 has risen significantly, to over 53,000 in the UK. The problems faced by such children include physical and sexual abuse as well as neglect.
- The higher risk of divorce and family breakdown puts children at higher risk of mental health issues.
- If current trends remain as they are, any child born today in the UK has more than a one-in-three chance of not living with both birth parents by the age of 15.
- The separation between childhood and adulthood is increasingly blurred. Through greater access to the internet and social media, children are increasingly exposed to what many would consider highly inappropriate material.
- The rise of social media sites has led to incidents of 'cyberbullying' and exploitation, and greater pressure to look a particular way.
- According to census figures there are estimated to be at least 376,000 young adult carers in the UK aged 16–25. They face considerable stress, including a higher likelihood of mental health problems, disrupted education and financial problems.
- Children are the objects of high-powered consumer campaigns. At a younger age this can lead to 'pester power' when they beg their parents to buy them particular goods, and at older ages young people can be under pressure to achieve a particular body shape and wear certain types of clothing and make-up.

Neil Postman (1982)

Postman believes that childhood is disappearing. He argues that this is due to the rise and fall of print media. In the past, children had to be able to read to access adult worlds, whereas now, children can access adult ideas and worlds through new forms of technology such as the internet and television, exposing them to adult realities.

Sue Palmer (2006)

Palmer argues that while new technologies are benefiting adults, changes in adult lifestyles have affected the way that children are looked after, both at home and at school. She says children's experiences are being 'polluted', leading to 'toxic childhood syndrome'.

Evaluation

- + March of progress views demonstrate many improvements in the life of children.
- + Conflict views draw attention to many contemporary problems affecting children and young people.
- – March of progress arguments ignore current problems such as child poverty, child abuse and exploitation.
- – Conflict views ignore some of the changes which have led to a more positive experience of childhood today.

> **Exam tip**
>
> Be careful not to use Ariès' study and ideas if you are being asked about childhood since 1900. Ariès' study relates to childhood in the seventeenth century.

> **Knowledge check 14**
>
> How might Ariès' research methodology be criticised?

> **Knowledge check 15**
>
> What is toxic childhood?

Social and cultural differences

There are considerable differences in the experience of childhood based on class, gender and ethnicity. For example, poorer children are less likely to do well at school, gendered socialisation may lead to very different expectations and outcomes for girls and boys, and cultural practices may mean childhood varies considerably among different ethnic groups.

Children's rights

In 1989, a number of governments around the world signed up to the United Nations Convention on the Rights of the Child. By 'child' is meant here everyone under the age of 18. The rights include, for example, respect for the views of the child; freedom of thought, belief and religion; and right to privacy.

The global picture

You may need to be aware of the ways in which the experience of childhood varies according to the cultural practices in a particular place. For example, in Sudan in Africa, children are recruited to be soldiers, a practice which would not occur in the UK. In many countries, the situation for many children is far worse than it is in the UK. Worldwide, millions of children are being brought up in abject poverty, with no access to adequate healthcare or education, and at work from a very young age.

Key concepts

childhood; social construct; march of progress views; toxic childhood; child-centred society

Knowledge check 16

What is meant by a child-centred society?

Exam tip

If a question asks specifically about the UK, or is obviously about the situation in the UK, you must focus your answer on that. However, there may be opportunities to demonstrate that you are aware of the wider, global picture with regard to children's rights.

Summary

- 'Childhood' is a social construct and its meaning varies according to time and place, and also within and between different groups.
- There are two main views about changes in childhood in Britain.
- The 'march of progress' view is that childhood has improved.
- The conflict view is that life has become more difficult for children.
- There are differences in the ways that parents from different groups bring up their children, but social class seems to exert a greater influence than ethnicity.
- Children now have a significant number of legal rights, but there are many cases of the abuse or denial of these rights.

■ Demographic changes since 1900 and the impact of globalisation

'**Demography**' is the study of populations and demographic trends are those changes in things that affect the composition of a population. These include birth and death rates, how long people are expected to live, the proportion of males and females, and migration both into and out of the country.

Birth rates

The birth rates in a population are influenced by many things, including the number of women of childbearing age. Overall, UK birth rates have fallen steadily since 1900. Exceptions are the two 'baby booms' after each of the two world wars.

Measuring birth rates

There are different ways to measure the births occurring in a society. The first is the **birth rate**, which is the number of live births per thousand of the total population in a given year. An alternative measure is the **fertility rate**, which records the number of live births per thousand women of childbearing age in a given year. Yet another measure is the **total fertility rate**, which is the total number of children a woman is likely to have during her childbearing years. Recently statisticians have been exploring conception rates.

Recent trends

- According to *The Lancet*, the birth rate in 2017 was 1.7, which is similar to that of most European countries.
- Fertility rates have decreased for every age group in 2017, except for women aged 40 years and over — in that age group, the rate increased by 1.3% to 16.1 births per 1,000 women, reaching the highest level since 1949.
- Changes in social norms are reflected in the fact that the average age of mothers giving birth in 2017 increased to 30.5 years, from 26.4 years in 1975.
- In 2017, just over half of all live births were to parents who were married or in a civil partnership (51.9%); however, 67.3% of live births outside of marriage or civil partnership were to parents who lived together.
- In 2017, 28.4% of live births were to mothers born outside the UK, following a gradual rise from 11.6% in 1990.
- In 2017, the total fertility rate (TFR) declined for the fifth consecutive year to 1.76 children per woman, from 1.81 in 2016.

Reasons for the fall in birth rates

- *The rising age of mothers.* The older a woman is before she has her first child, the fewer children she is likely to have. Older mothers also find it more difficult to conceive.

- *The survival of children.* In 1900, before the welfare state, poorer families especially needed to have some surviving children to care for ageing parents. As more children survived, the need to have as many offspring fell.
- *Economic cost.* Children used to be an economic asset for their family, earning wages from a very early age. As the age of compulsory education has risen, children have increasingly become an economic cost, making it more difficult for families to support large numbers of children. Figures published in 2015 by the Centre for Economics and Business Research show that the cost of raising a child to the age of 21 has risen by 63% since 2003 and stands at about £230,000 per child, with the first four years of life being the most expensive.
- *Improved availability and reliability of contraception.* The contraceptive pill was made available on the NHS in 1961, though initially only to married women who had already borne children. In 1974, it was made available on prescription to single women.
- *Legalised abortion.* Women have always resorted to abortion, often at devastating cost to themselves. From 1967, under certain conditions, abortion was made legal in England, Wales and Scotland.
- *Women's increased participation in the labour market.* While many mothers are in paid employment, this is obviously more difficult for mothers with larger families.
- *The growing number of women who remain childless.* Of women born in 1968 (i.e. whose childbearing years are thought to be over), 18% are childless, compared with 11% of women born in 1941.

Knowledge check 17

What is the difference in meaning between the birth rate and the fertility rate?

Exam tip

As with many other demographic trends, show that you are aware that the overall figures disguise differences between groups, particularly differences in social class, ethnic group and religion.

Death rates

The deaths in a population are measured by the **death rate**, sometimes referred to as the mortality rate. This is affected by the **age distribution of the population**. The current UK death rate is 9.34; in 1900 it was around 16. The term 'mortality rate' is usually applied when the deaths among a particular section of the population are being measured, such as among infants, women in childbirth, or people in specific age groups.

The largest fall in death rates since 1900 has been among infants and children. Death rates among this group fell to low levels by 1950. Adult death rates fell more slowly. The greatest fall in mortality among people of advanced ages has occurred since the 1970s.

Death rates vary by social class, with higher rates of premature death among working-class people.

Death rate The number of deaths per thousand of the population in a given year.

Age distribution of the population The proportion of people in different age groups throughout the population.

Infant mortality rate (IMR)

This measures the number of babies who die before their first birthday per thousand live births in a given year. The IMR is often used as a general measure of the health of a population. In the UK, it has been falling steadily since 1900, though there were increases during the depression of the 1920s and 1930s, and during the Second World War. The rate now stands at 3.8, whereas in 1900 it was 140. Half of all babies who died in 1900 did so as a result of infectious diseases such as measles, whooping cough and diphtheria.

Exam tip

Show that you know that the IMR is one measure that shows a clear difference between social classes.

Reasons for the fall in death rates

Reasons for the fall in death rates include:

- advances in medicine, both in diagnosis and treatment, with particular advances in surgery
- significant improvements in public health, sanitation, housing and the supply of clean water
- programmes of vaccination, which have had a particularly beneficial effect on infants and children, and have helped significantly to reduce death rates from infectious diseases
- the introduction of the National Health Service in 1947, providing free treatment and care
- the development of antibiotics
- improvements in ante-natal and post-natal care
- improved food production and a generally higher standard of living
- changes in the law resulting in safer working conditions, though there are still some occupations that are particularly hazardous

Family size

Family size has been decreasing steadily on average since 1900. The combined effect of fewer babies being born and increased life expectancy means an increase in the **dependency ratio**. This means that the earnings of each person of working age have to support an increased number of dependants.

There are exceptions to the general rule of falling family size.

Muslim families

According to the Pew Research Center (2017), the Muslim population of the UK is set to triple in 30 years. The number of Muslim people in the country would rise from 4.1 million in 2016 to 13 million in 2050. The UK also has one of the largest gaps in fertility rates between Muslims and non-Muslims: Muslim women have an average of 2.9 children while the figure for non-Muslims is 1.8. This suggests that the UK will have the highest overall population of Muslim people in the EU, at 13 million, making up 16.7% of the population.

Muslims are ethnically diverse, coming from a wide range of backgrounds. According to an Ipsos MORI survey (2018), the Muslim population in the UK is younger than the rest of the UK population, with one in three Muslim people being 15 or younger. Also, Muslim families are more likely to contain both biological parents of children — this is true of 77% of Muslim 13–14-year-olds, whereas only 63% of non-Muslims have their natural father in the household. Muslim couples are less likely to divorce and are likely to have stronger ties with extended family.

Reasons for the change in family size

Couples are delaying having their first child, meaning that the potential childbearing period is shortened. The economic cost of raising a child means that many couples delay having a second child or decide to have only one child. Women's greater participation in the labour market contributes both to the delay in starting a family

> **Knowledge check 18**
> Why is the family getting smaller on average?

> **Dependency ratio**
> The ratio of the number of dependent people (those not of working age, i.e. 0–15 and 65-plus) to the number of people of working age.

> **Exam tip**
> Remember the variations in family size among different social class, religious and ethnic groups.

and to the decision to limit the number of children, due to the difficulties of being a working parent.

Life expectancy and an ageing population

There has been a more or less continuous rise in **life expectancy** since 1900. In 1900, life expectancy at birth was 47 for males and 50 for females. Half of all deaths occurred to those under 45. In 2017, according to the Office for National Statistics, life expectancy at birth in England has now increased to 79.6 years for males and 83.2 years for females. People are living longer than at the start of the century, but since 2011 the rate of increase in life expectancy has slowed for both sexes.

Increased life expectancy, when combined with low fertility rates, leads to an ageing population. This has important consequences for society as a whole:

- *Welfare payments* — as more people will be drawing their pensions and may also be in need of other benefits, this will increase the pressure on the welfare system.
- *Retirement age* — partly in order to fund this, the age at which people can retire from work and draw a pension will rise.
- *Health and social care* — older people increasingly have various health conditions and need medication and hospital care more frequently than younger people. This will put a strain on the NHS and social services.
- *Accommodation* — there will be a growing need for places in care homes and assisted living facilities for those unable to look after themselves.
- *Family carers* — at least in the initial stages of a person's physical and/or mental decline, family members provide at least some care. The number of those caring for elderly relatives will increase.
- *Politics* — older people tend to have a higher voting turn-out rate than younger people, which might have an effect on the policies that parties offer.
- *Support* — by no means all older people need care and support. Many of them provide invaluable help to younger members of their family, for example in childcare and financial support.

It is important to remember that older people make many positive contributions, including grandparents playing a more important role in their grandchildren's lives as well as older people now contributing more to the economy.

Reasons for the increase in life expectancy

There is no single reason for the steady increase in life expectancy, but the following have all been contributory factors:

- advances in medicine, especially in surgery and the control of infectious diseases
- improvements in sanitation and housing
- improvements in food supply and quality
- the introduction of the welfare state and the National Health Service
- new drugs to cure or to extend the life of those with once-fatal diseases, such as some types of cancer
- improvements in health education and preventive medicine, giving people the knowledge to live a healthy lifestyle

Life expectancy The average age to which people are expected to live. Life expectancy can be measured at any age — for example at birth, at the start of adulthood and at the start of old age.

Knowledge check 19

What is meant by 'an ageing population'?

Exam tip

Remember that there are social class differences in life expectancy.

Migration and globalisation

Migration refers to the flow of people in and out of a country, usually measured in thousands per year. Immigration refers to the number of people coming into a country to live and work, while emigration refers to those leaving a country. The difference between these two figures is known as net migration. Net migration figures are important as they give an idea about changes in population size.

Exam tip

Always remember when asked about 'migration' that it refers to both immigrants and emigrants.

Demographic impact of migration

Populations are likely to grow if there is a high proportion of foreign-born female immigrants of childbearing age, and if fertility rates in the country of origin are higher than in the host country. Both of these factors occur in UK immigration patterns, thus contributing to population growth.

Who are the migrants?

Immigration can be difficult to measure accurately, but the Office for National Statistics estimates that around 270,000 more people came to the UK than left in the year ending March 2018, so long-term net migration has continued to add to the UK population.

The net migration rate, which is the difference between the number of immigrants and the number of emigrants throughout the year, has fallen from the peak levels seen in 2015 and 2016 and has remained broadly stable since. Underlying this period of stability, long-term immigration and long-term emigration have remained broadly stable at around 610,000 and 340,000 respectively in the year ending March 2018. Most immigrants in 2016 came from Poland, followed by Romania, Ireland, Italy and then Portugal.

Exam tip

It is very important to acknowledge the positive contribution of immigrants to the UK economy and culture.

Why do people come to the UK?

Apart from British-born citizens returning home after living abroad, the most common reasons for people coming to the UK are as follows:

- *Work* — the most common reason non-British citizens reported for coming to the UK in 2016 was work. About 226,000 (50%) came for work, followed by those who came for study (124,000 or 27%).
- *Study* — a very large number of foreign-born young people come to the UK to study, but their stay is almost always temporary.
- *Joining a family member* — the rules have been tightened. Only British citizens or those resident in the UK earning a particular gross annual salary set by the government can apply to allow their spouse, partner, fiancé(e) or child(ren) to enter and live in the UK.
- *Asylum* — asylum seekers represent only a very small proportion of immigrants, as the rules granting them permission to stay are very strict.

Knowledge check 20

State what is meant by 'net migration'.

How does globalisation affect family life?

Globalisation refers to the increasing integration and interdependence of countries and their economies, societies, cultures, politics and technology. Globalisation has had profound effects in recent years due to increasing ease of transport and travel along with the increasing role of technology in people's lives. Globalisation has had many effects on the family, in terms of people's roles, relationships and family structures. Examples include the following:

- Many people are now expected to travel for work, resulting in some couples living apart together (LAT).
- Increased use of technology has made it possible for families and extended families to maintain contact, despite not living near to each other.
- More families are likely to move due to the increased ease and availability of travel, so families are even more geographically mobile than before.
- Immigration has increased as travel and transport have become easier, leading to greater cultural diversity in the UK, including a variety of differences such as in fertility rates and in family structures, roles and relationships.

Knowledge check 21

Identify two effects of immigration on family structures.

Key concepts

demography; birth rate; fertility rate; death rate; mortality rate; infant mortality rate; life expectancy; ageing population; migration; globalisation

Summary

- With a few exceptions, birth rates have fallen steadily since 1900.
- A growing proportion of births are now to women born outside the UK.
- The largest fall in death rates occurred among babies and young children. Adult death rates fell more slowly.
- Life expectancy has increased considerably, with the result that the UK has an ageing population.
- Migrants tend to be younger and to come to the UK to work or study, and the women tend to have higher fertility rates than UK-born women.
- Globalisation has resulted in more travel and increased use of information technology, leading to significant changes in family life.

Beliefs in society

■ Ideology, science and religion

In this topic, you need to be aware of three belief systems: ideology, science and religion. Each of these emerged at specific times in particular social contexts. You will need to be aware of the characteristics of each belief system and know about examples of each, as well as understanding how each belief system relates to the others.

Ideology

An ideology is a set of ideas and beliefs held by an individual, group or society which reflects their needs or aspirations and which is used to make sense of their world. Many important ideologies are political and/or economic, such as Marxism or conservatism. Ideologies are used to guide or inform people's behaviour. Ideologies do not rely on empirical evidence (although they may refer to it) and they do not involve belief in any form of supernatural being. For example, feminists believe that women are oppressed by society and the role of feminism is to challenge patriarchy to improve the lives of women.

Science

The term 'science' refers both to a method of enquiry and to a particular body of knowledge, such as chemistry or physics. It is characterised by the following:

- It uses a scientific method of enquiry, which aims to discover regularities and recurring relationships between variables by a rigorous system of observation and the collection of empirical evidence.
- It proceeds through **hypothesis** formation and controlled testing, with the aim of identifying theories (confirmed hypotheses) and eventually scientific laws.
- The main goal is to understand the natural world in order to make predictions and, where possible, to control it.
- Science is an **open knowledge system**, which means that findings can be tested and falsified, being replaced by new ideas or empirical evidence.

Hypothesis A testable statement, to be proven or disproven.

Open knowledge system A system such as science where knowledge can be challenged, falsified and replaced with new knowledge.

What is the relationship between science and religion?

Some see religion and science as incompatible with each other, and there are examples of conflict, for instance between those whose religious beliefs include the idea of creationism (that the Bible story of God creating the world in six days is literally true) and the scientific beliefs and evidence regarding evolution. However, research suggests that almost a half of scientists hold some religious beliefs and see no problem with this.

Knowledge check 22

By what term is the scientific method of enquiry generally known?

- One of the first major conflicts between the Christian church and science occurred in the sixteenth and seventeenth centuries, when Copernicus and Galileo claimed that the sun was at the centre of the universe, and that the Earth and other planets moved around it. Religious thinkers of the time saw this view as highly controversial because it directly challenged religious beliefs — according to the Bible, the Earth was the centre.
- A more serious scientific challenge to the authority of the church was Darwin's theory of evolution, and this continues to cause controversy today, between those accepting Darwinian theory and creationists, who hold that the Bible stories of the Earth's creation are literally true.
- With the spread of the **Enlightenment** and scientific views, many former teachings of the church have been changed or dropped, and it is suggested that only the church's core teachings remain intact. The current situation tends to be that the church is the authority on moral and spiritual issues, while science deals with factual matters.

Enlightenment A shift in society from believing in religion to more rational ways of thinking, largely as a result of the spread of ideas through the print press.

Religion

Broadly speaking, what we term 'religion' refers to a set of ideas and beliefs relating to the supernatural world, dealing with questions such as the meaning of life and death and what happens after death, and also providing a moral code that states how one should live one's life.

There is no single accepted definition of what we mean by 'religion'. Nevertheless, definitions are important because they are used to decide what should be examined as a religious phenomenon and what should be excluded. The definition adopted will lead sociologists to ask different questions about the nature, scale and importance of religious belief and activity in society, often leading them to different conclusions.

Some of the most important types of definition are:

- **Inclusivist definitions**: these include many phenomena that to some might seem controversial, such as magic, or even beliefs some might consider non-religious beliefs, such as veganism.
- **Exclusivist definitions**: these exclude phenomena that make no reference to a supernatural being or beings, and therefore limit what will be defined as religious. Stark and Bainbridge (1985) use an exclusivist definition of religion when they argue that religions must involve some conception of a supernatural being, world or force, and the notion that events and conditions on Earth are influenced by the supernatural.

There are also substantive or functional definitions:

- **Substantive definitions**: these refer to a defining characteristic, such as a belief in God, as the distinctive feature of a religion.
- **Functional definitions**: these focus on the role that religion performs for society as a whole, such as acting as a unifying force.

Finally, there is the **social constructionist definition** of religion, which focuses on what religion means to the individual person.

Evaluation

- + It is important to explore different definitions of religion because they affect the way that religion is measured.
- − Inclusivist-functional definitions are so encompassing that they make the idea of a specifically religious sphere of activity difficult to identify — everything can be seen as 'religious'.
- − Exclusivist-substantive definitions limit what can be seen as religious and lead inevitably to the idea that in many societies religious observance has declined in importance.

What is the role of religion?

There is much debate about the role or function that religion fulfils, both for the individual and for society. You will be expected to discuss the strengths and weaknesses of each theory in helping us to understand the function of religion in contemporary society.

Functionalist views

Functionalists argue that religion plays an important role in socialising both adults and children. They believe that individuals need socialising in order for society to function. Religion therefore has a specific purpose to remind people of particular core shared values, as well as to encourage people to feel that they are part of society.

Knowledge check 23

Explain two ways in which science challenges religious beliefs.

Exam tip

It is always a good idea to show that you know when each belief system emerged, with religion being the earliest belief system and ideologies and science appearing more recently.

Exam tip

Make sure that you know what type of theory you are writing about. Remember the assumptions that each type of theory makes, depending if it is consensus, conflict, structure or action.

Durkheim

Durkheim (1858–1917), a founding father of sociology, focused on the positive role religion plays as an essential part of the shared consciousness ('conscience collective') that makes societies function.

■ He argued that there is a difference between 'the profane', which was normal, everyday life, and 'the sacred', which referred to what he called things 'set apart and forbidden'.

■ He studied the totemism of Aboriginal Australians, a form of religion in which the sacred object of the totem represented the clan or tribe. In this way the totem symbolised society, and the collective rituals restated the importance and significance of shared social bonds.

■ Religion thus acted to bind individuals to society, enabling them to understand and accept approved social relationships through the shared values of religious belief.

■ Religion also served to regulate people's behaviour by providing moral guidance, which enabled people to live together in society without the problems caused by selfish individualism.

Malinowski

Malinowski (1925) focused on the individual psychological functions of religion.

■ He saw religion as the response of individuals to the uncertainty of the world, providing them with a sense of security.

■ In his research on the Trobriand Islands, Malinowski established that people use religion as a way of coping with situations where there is a high level of risk, for example fishing in dangerous waters.

Talcott Parsons

Parsons (1949) agreed with Durkheim that the shared moral values arising from religious beliefs help to maintain a stable society.

■ He saw religion as continuing to fulfil some of the 'needs' of society.

■ Parsons argued that religion operates as a 'mechanism of adjustment', meaning it is somewhere to turn when there are 'life crises' which may potentially disrupt people's lives and therefore social order.

Bellah

More recently, Bellah (1967) reinforced earlier functionalist beliefs, arguing that religion continues to perform essential social functions although perhaps not through traditional religious institutions.

■ Bellah introduced the concept of 'civil religion', by which he meant the adoption of religious ideas, rituals and symbols to bind society together.

■ His ideas were developed with regard to American society, though they are now applied more widely. Some examples would be pledging allegiance to the flag and US presidents ending their speeches with the words 'God bless America'. Others have suggested that Armistice Day commemorations, coronations and the response to the death of Diana, Princess of Wales, are also examples of civil religion.

Knowledge check 24

Provide an example of how a religious funeral may act as a 'mechanism of adjustment'.

Key concepts

'conscience collective'; core values; sacred and profane; shared rituals; moral guidance; mechanism of adjustment; civil religion

Evaluation

- ■ + Religion plays an important role in the establishment and maintenance of social cohesion.
- ■ + Religion benefits the individual and society through offering comfort, therefore reducing the chance of instability.
- ■ − This is a static view of religion — functionalists did not attempt to explain the rise of new religions.
- ■ − The evidence for Durkheim's and Malinowski's views came from the study of very small, atypical societies which cannot easily be applied to complex, religiously diverse contemporary societies.
- ■ − Traditional functionalist theories are unable to account for secularisation or the conflict resulting from religious beliefs.

Exam tip

Make sure that you can distinguish between the views of Durkheim and those of other functionalist writers on religion.

Knowledge check 25

Give an example of how religion may cause conflict in contemporary society.

Marxist views

Marxists believe that religion reflects and maintains capitalist ideology. Marxists argue that ideas are a reflection of economic relations of production, whereby the ruling class seek to exploit the working class in their pursuit of profit. Marxists claim that religion is part of the superstructure, where ideas are developed which encourage the working class to accept their position and not challenge it.

Marx

For Marx (1818–1883), religion was built by society, a social construct. 'Man makes religion, religion doesn't make man.' In particular, religion is the product of those in power — those who control the economy, the ruling class or bourgeoisie. Marx argued that there were two main functions of religion:

- ■ Marx saw religion as acting as a cushion to the effects of capitalism, to offer comfort, or in his words to act as an 'opium of the masses'. In this way religion prevents people from challenging the system and therefore maintains capitalism.
- ■ Marx saw religion as an aspect of ideology which was an important element in the '**false consciousness**' of both the working class (or proletariat) and the bourgeoisie, in that neither group had a real appreciation of their position as pawns of the system. Religion blinds the working class to their true condition, i.e. one of exploitation, and socialises them into a set of beliefs that is contrary to their interests. In particular, it teaches them that obedience to authority ('accepting God's will') is their route to salvation, which will await them in the afterlife. This is sometimes known as the 'theodicy of disprivilege', whereby inequalities are explained as God-given and therefore cannot and should not be challenged.

False consciousness
A term used by Marx to describe the beliefs, particularly of the proletariat, that did not reflect their actual position (one of exploitation) but came from ruling-class ideology. False consciousness prevented members of the working class from seeing their 'true' class position.

Knowledge check 26

Marx wrote that religion is 'the opium of the people'. Briefly explain what is meant by this.

Key concepts

bourgeoisie; proletariat; false consciousness; ideology

Evaluation

- ■ + Religion is seen as being determined by the economic base (substructure) rather than theological ideas.
- ■ + There is an acknowledgement that for the proletariat, religion can help to ease the pain of exploitation.
- ■ + The idea that the bourgeoisie are carrying out God's will enables them to continue their pursuit of profit and exploitation of the proletariat.
- ■ − The explanation of religion is that its sole origin is the economic base of society.
- ■ − Marx may have overstated the role of religion in ruling-class ideology.
- ■ − Marx's ideas may no longer be relevant in a contemporary society where there are a range of belief systems and secularisation coexisting.

Neo-Marxism

Neo-Marxist writers have taken a less deterministic view of religion than Marx and have acknowledged that religious ideas could sometimes act as a force for social change to benefit the working class.

Gramsci

Gramsci (1971) used the concept of **hegemony** to show how some of society's institutions, including religion, can shape people's beliefs and perceptions of the world. However, it is almost impossible to maintain complete hegemonic control, so there is always the possibility that the dominant ideas of the ruling class could be challenged.

Maduro

Maduro (1982) also believes that the role of religion is more complex than Marx suggested, and that at certain periods religion can be relatively autonomous rather than always supporting and preserving the status quo. Maduro explores examples in Latin America where for a brief period of time, religious leaders challenged the unfair practices in society, a process he calls liberation theology.

Hegemony In this context, refers to the situation in which a dominant group controls subservient groups not by force but by particular ideas. Thus, persuading the working class that an unequal society is normal and can be justified by religious beliefs allows members of the bourgeoisie to rule without the constant threat of revolution.

Evaluation

- ■ + Acknowledges that religion can sometimes act independently of the substructure.
- ■ + Shows how religion can sometimes benefit the working class, for example through liberation theology.
- ■ + Accepts that the ruling class cannot always achieve complete hegemonic control.
- ■ − Can overstate the revolutionary aspects of religion — in most cases, it is used to support the status quo and helps to preserve the power of the ruling class.

Interactionism

Interactionism looks at the micro aspects of religion, i.e. how it relates to individuals and individual experiences. In other words, it looks at what religion does for the individual.

Like Marx, interactionists see religion as a social construct, developed and maintained by individual beliefs. They argue that religion provides a framework for interpreting and understanding the world; it gives people categories and concepts that help them to make sense of the world, and helps to provide answers to the existential questions of life, death, joy and suffering.

Interactionism focuses on the meaning that individuals give to things. Ideas and practices are not sacred unless and until people believe them to be, and only then do they take on special significance and bring meaning to people's lives.

Objects and symbols are considered to possess power and provide meanings that are opposed to the chaos that confronts individuals as they try to make sense of their life. According to Berger (1984), some people and objects are cloaked by the '**sacred canopy**', which gives them special power and meanings.

Weber (1905), a well-known founder of the interpretivist approach, argues that a shift in the meanings connected to religion can lead to wider changes in society, as he demonstrates through his study of the emergence of Calvinism in Germany (see p. 42 for more detail).

Evaluation

- ■ + Interactionists are interested in the small-scale meanings attached to religious beliefs, which may be more useful than structural explanations.
- ■ + Weber stressed the importance of individual beliefs as factors in social developments, rejecting economic determinism.
- ■ − Interactionists ignore the influence of structural factors when considering the role of religion.
- ■ − Interactionists are unable to account for the larger-scale changes in beliefs.

Postmodernism

A key feature of postmodernism is the belief in the end of 'metanarratives', the so-called 'big ideas' of science and religion. However, many see religion as a source of reassurance and moral guidance in societies increasingly characterised by insecurities brought about by the loosening of kinship and community ties and the increase in individual freedom and choice.

Bauman (2005) links postmodernity to the decline of certainty, authority and objectivity, and the rise of 'neo-tribalism'. This refers to new ways of 'belonging' to groups, based on often temporary shared interests rather than the traditional links of kinship, community and religion.

Exam tip

Make sure that you explain how interactionism differs in approach from other theories, as an agency-based theory rather than a structural theory.

Sacred canopy A term used by Berger to describe the way in which religious beliefs provide an overarching system of meaning to help people understand and explain the world.

Exam tip

When studying theories of religion, it is a good idea to make a list showing those areas where different theories agree with one or more others.

Knowledge check 27

Explain why people may no longer believe in a single metanarrative in postmodern society.

Giddens (2000) develops the concept of 'disembedding' to refer to the ways in which cultural practices and social relationships are taken from their original context and combined with other practices and relationships at different times and in different places. An example of this is the way that some elements of Eastern philosophies and practices such as yoga and meditation have been incorporated into some 'New Age' beliefs.

Lyon (1999) believes that ideas of secularisation are misplaced and says that the evidence shows there is a 're-enchantment of the world', and that religion can flourish in postmodern conditions.

In a postmodern world of endless choice and uncertainty, some see the rise of **religious fundamentalism** (see p. 43) as a rational response to 'choice overload', where individuals have to make choices not only among consumer products but also among ideas and values. Fundamentalism offers a return to certainties.

Key concepts
metanarratives; choice; fundamentalism; disembedding

Evaluation
- + Offers an explanation for the increase in the number and nature of religious groups in contemporary society, including sects, cults and New Age practices.
- + Sees the rise of fundamentalism as a rational response to the lack of certainty in postmodern societies.
- − Overemphasises the extent to which the old certainties and ideas have collapsed and the degree to which people are faced with 'real' choices.
- − Fundamentalism can be seen as a reactionary response to modernism, rather than a postmodern reaction to increased choice.

Feminist perspectives
There are several feminist perspectives on religion, but they tend to view most religions as patriarchal institutions, asserting the power of males over females. This claim is based on examining religious beliefs and texts and the roles allocated to women within religious institutions.

However, there are a small number of women for whom religion is liberating. For example, Watson (1994) and Woodhead (2002) found that wearing the veil enabled some Muslim women to feel liberated from the male gaze. Other women argue that religion provides a particular form of status, such as being a powerful figure in family life in Judaism. Finally, women may gain a great deal of support within religious communities.

Most feminists start from the view that what we know of ancient religions indicates that they celebrated what was regarded as the mystical power of women, and there were powerful female goddesses and priestesses. Male-dominated religions such as Christianity, Islam and Judaism are believed to have suppressed the older, female-orientated religions and relegated women to lesser, subservient roles.

Religious fundamentalism A belief that there is a need to return to what are regarded as the original beliefs and practices of the religion, usually thought to reside in the sacred texts, such as the Bible, the Torah, the Talmud and the Qur'an.

Exam tip

Showing that there is no single agreed position within a particular perspective is a good way of demonstrating the skills of analysis and evaluation.

Exam tip

Remember that there have been changes in some religions with regard to the role of women. For example, the Church of England now has ordained female ministers and female bishops, while Judaism has female rabbis.

Knowledge check 28

Give an example, from any religion with which you are familiar, of a position that is forbidden to women.

Aldridge (2007) has pointed out how few religions treat men and women equally. Those that might be able to claim this include the Religious Society of Friends (Quakers), Unitarians and Christian Scientists. He also points out that when the subservient role of women is challenged, the practices tend to be justified in terms of charismatic or traditional authority. Thus arguments based on the right of women to equal treatment are regarded as of lesser importance than justifications based on sacred texts.

Bruce (2002) points out that all religions have at the heart of their teachings a profound interest in sexuality and the family. He argues that after centuries of defending and explaining particular patterns of gender relations, religions find it difficult to change their position. He points out that since it is usually within the family that religious beliefs and traditions are passed down the generations, it is easy to see why fundamentalists in particular would be opposed to changes in gender roles.

Perhaps because of these traditional patterns, many new religious movements (NRMs) (see p. 47) have a particular appeal for women. Many NRMs and New Age movements offer women more powerful and liberating roles than do traditional religions and promote positive images of womanhood. Some of these movements also encourage men to explore the more 'feminine' side of their nature.

(see p. 47)

Exam tip

Make a list of some religious teachings (ideally from more than one religion) that are concerned with sexuality and the family. Lists such as this are very useful when revising, as they provide examples with which to illustrate your arguments and evidence.

Key concepts

patriarchy; oppression; liberal and radical feminism; roles within religion

Evaluation

- + Feminist perspectives draw attention to the patriarchal nature of most religions.
- + Offer some explanation of the continued subservient roles allocated to women within religions.
- + Suggest why more women than men might be attracted to NRMs.
- – Feminist perspectives don't really explain why the older, female-oriented religions were suppressed.
- – Tend to ignore the positive role that religion can play for women, for example in offering support and status within the role in the family.

Summary

- There are three belief systems: religion, ideology and science.
- Science refers to both a body of knowledge and a method of developing and testing hypotheses.
- When looking at any hypotheses, research or writings on religion, it is important to note which definition of religion is being used.
- Different theories of religion take different viewpoints on the relationship between religion, religious beliefs and the wider society.

■ Religion, social change and social stability

Religion and social change

There is an important debate within sociology regarding whether religion acts, or under certain circumstances can act, as a force for social change, or whether it is primarily a conservative force, helping to maintain the status quo.

Knowledge check 29

Briefly explain what is meant by the 'status quo'.

The ideas of Max Weber and the relationship between Calvinist beliefs and modern capitalism are particularly important in showing how religion can act to bring about social change. In his 1905 paper entitled 'The Protestant ethic and the spirit of capitalism', Weber argued that the transition to Calvinism led to a change in the meanings held by people which resulted in the emergence of capitalism. There were three particular meanings which became important:

- *ascetic lifestyle* (living frugally)
- *work as a calling* (the idea that being hard-working was a sign of being religiously good)
- *predestination* (the idea that it is already decided whether a person will go to heaven or not, which caused people to look anxiously for signs of God's favour, such as economic success)

Weber's arguments were useful since they were among the first to take an interpretivist approach which focuses on the ways in which small-scale meanings can lead to significant changes in wider society. He was later criticised for overlooking the fact that capitalism emerged in other parts of the world in different contexts.

Other examples of situations where religion can be argued to have been instrumental in bringing about social change include the following:

- The civil rights movement in the USA in the 1960s was closely linked with the black preacher Martin Luther King.
- In Latin America in the 1960s and 1970s, radical and even revolutionary groups emerged within the Roman Catholic Church and some priests and nuns took the side of the poor and oppressed against right-wing leaderships. This is referred to as **liberation theology**.
- Islamic fundamentalists brought down the Westernised rule of the Shah of Persia in 1979 and replaced it with the world's first Islamic state, Iran, governed by ayatollahs (high-ranking Shiite religious leaders). A return to conservative values was enforced.
- In the 1980s, the Roman Catholic Church in Poland opposed the Communist regime and supported the Solidarity trade union movement to achieve social change.

Liberation theology A belief that people have a duty to free themselves from social, economic and political oppression in this world, rather than accepting such injustices as divine will.

Exam tip

You may be asked if religion leads to social change, or if it prevents or inhibits social change. You may also be asked to what extent religion leads to stability or instability, which is a different question. Be aware of the differences in wording of the questions.

Key concepts

Protestant ethic; predestination; ascetic lifestyle; work as a calling; liberation theology; Islamic fundamentalism; civil rights movement

Evaluation

- ▪ + Examples show that under certain circumstances, religions and religious ideas can help to bring about social change.
- ▪ + Some religious ideas do challenge the status quo.
- ▪ – It can be argued that these are minority examples and that, in general, the established churches act in the interests of the most powerful group(s) to maintain the existing social order.

Religion and social conflict

Where religion is associated with social change, it is often involved in social conflict. Increasingly, global tensions highlight the capacity of religions to threaten or challenge the prevailing social order, often resulting in conflict.

The huge tensions between Israel and Palestine are at least in part the result of conflicts between Jews and Muslims. Tensions between Hindus and Muslims in India have resulted in recent episodes of violent conflict. Similarly, the long history of conflict between Protestants and Catholics in Northern Ireland has its roots in ethnic and political divisions as well as in religious differences.

An aspect of religious beliefs particularly associated with conflict is religious fundamentalism (see key term definition on p. 40). Fundamentalism is a rejection of modernity, with a strong desire to impose what are regarded as the traditional beliefs on the whole of society. Some fundamentalist groups reject the liberal values of contemporary society, objecting for instance to women working, sex outside marriage and homosexuality. It is accepted that 'unbelievers' are found not only outside the faith but also within it. Fundamentalist movements can be regarded as inherently totalitarian, in that they seek to make all aspects of society conform to religious laws.

Even though fundamentalist groups are against modernity, they often use modern technologies to spread their message.

Fundamentalists can be found in many different religions. Fundamentalist movements exist in Christianity, Islam, Judaism, Hinduism and Sikhism. Many, however, see fundamentalism not only as an aspect of traditional religiosity but also as an inherently political movement, often involving, and of particular appeal to, those members of a society who are, or who consider themselves to be, socially, economically or politically oppressed.

Fundamentalism may be expressed in different ways. Some fundamentalists try to bring about social change through political means, such as the right-wing Christian **evangelicals** (sometimes referred to as the New Christian Right) allied to the American Republican Party, who oppose what they see as wrongful social policies such as gay rights, same-sex marriage and access to abortion.

Knowledge check 30

Give an example of a modern technology platform used by a fundamentalist group.

Evangelical Christians
Believe in living their life as far as possible in accordance with the New Testament gospels. They accept the Bible as the sole source of religious authority and believe that salvation is possible only by conversion and spiritual regeneration — being 'born again'.

Other fundamentalist groups are associated with often violent conflicts. Examples include militant religious Zionists in Israel, Hamas in Palestine, the Lord's Resistance Army in Uganda, Boko Haram in Nigeria, al-Qaeda and the Islamic State in the Middle East.

Evaluation

- + Can be seen as a reaction against postmodernity in which all metanarratives have been undermined.
- + Can be seen as a challenge to established religious beliefs and practices, invoking a re-examination of the founding texts.
- + Represents an authentic religious response to increasing secularisation.
- − The term 'fundamentalism' was originally used to refer to a movement in American Protestantism — it is not necessarily appropriate to apply it to other, especially non-Western, religions.
- − Some people question the extent to which fundamentalism has actually grown. The very visible nature of some events may make such movements seem more numerous and powerful than they actually are.

Exam tip

Showing that you recognise that there are different types of fundamentalist groups will demonstrate knowledge, analysis and evaluation. For example, there are fundamentalist groups which act peacefully.

Religion and social stability

The idea that religion brings, or can bring, social stability is related to functionalist ideas that religion serves to integrate the members of society into a shared value system. However, it goes further by claiming that religion seeks to defend the political and social status quo. In this view, religion is an essentially conservative force in society.

The relationship between religion and social stability is at least partly based on the links in many societies between the state and a specific religion. In such cases, the established religion is often granted certain privileges, and there are usually connections between leading political and religious leaders. The established, or state, church in England is the Church of England, with the reigning monarch as the Supreme Governor.

Knowledge check 31

Give an example of how some members of the Church of England have formal political power.

It is sometimes suggested that it is the very conservatism of many religions that draws people to them, as the freedom and individuality of postmodern society leave them searching for stability. It is worth noting that it is not always easy to fit a particular religious movement into a particular category. Examples such as the Iranian revolution, Islamic State and the Taliban can be seen as radical and revolutionary in their attempts to bring about religious and political change, but also as conservative in their desire to make their societies return to what are seen as traditional values.

Key concepts

status quo; established religion; conservatism

Evaluation

- + The emphasis on tradition and continuity has a wide appeal in conditions of rapid change.
- + State religions link religious beliefs and practices to allegiance to the state, helping to explain the absence of revolutionary movements.
- – Conservative religious bodies have been allied to certain nation states and this has led them to defend and support ruthless regimes and practices that ignore human rights.
- – Unquestioning support for the status quo hampers progress in many areas of life, for example equal rights for women and gay people.
- – Clinging to traditional values in a changing world can cause much unhappiness, as people struggle to reconcile their religious faith with their preferred way of life.

Summary

- Religions and religious beliefs can act as a force for social change.
- They can also act to maintain social stability and preserve the status quo.
- Some religious groups are radical in that they attempt to overthrow a particular regime or set of values, but conservative in that once established, they attempt, sometimes by force, to bring that society back to 'traditional values'.
- Religions can also act as a source of social conflict, either between different religions or within the same religion.

Religious organisations

In order to study religious organisations and how they might differ in their structure, roles, beliefs and practices, sociologists have attempted to classify them into broad groups. This is helpful, but it is important to remember that often such classifications are 'rough guides' — what Weber would call 'ideal types' — and it is not always easy or even possible to place a particular group into one of the categories. Equally important is the fact that many classifications, particularly the earlier ones, were developed in respect of the Christian religion, and it is not easy, or often even helpful, to try to apply the distinctions to other religious faiths.

Max Weber and Ernst Troeltsch were the first sociologists to attempt a classification of religious organisations, and their distinction was between churches and sects. Sociologists since then have developed other classifications.

Knowledge check 32

Briefly explain what Weber meant by an 'ideal type'.

Churches

Churches are held to have the following characteristics:

- There is a formal organisational structure with a hierarchy of paid officials.
- Membership is open to everyone.
- Membership is usually 'ascribed' — that is, members are born into the church, though some will be converts. Being baptised into the church brings about 'salvation through grace'.

- They tend to be large and appeal to the middle class, especially the Church of England.
- They have positive attitudes towards, and often close links with, the state and the established order, sometimes resulting in ideologies to defend and legitimise the status quo.

Examples include the Roman Catholic Church and the Church of England.

Sects

The term 'sect' covers a wide variety of religious organisations. Their nature has changed over time, but again, an attempt has been made to find common characteristics.

Many early sects emerged as direct challenges to the established church, as schismatic or splinter groups that disagreed with certain doctrines. They were often protesting against what they saw as 'modernising' influences. Stark and Bainbridge (1973) said that 'sects claim to be authentic, purged versions of the faith from which they split'.

Characteristics of sects include the following:
- At least initially, they tend to be small, and are often led by a charismatic leader.
- They hold a belief that only their members will be 'saved' through their personal commitment and adherence to a particular lifestyle — 'salvation through faith'.
- Membership is often through a personal spiritual experience.
- Members often have to adhere to a strict moral code.
- Members are often drawn from the lower social classes and marginalised groups.
- There is sometimes an oppositional relationship to the state.

Given the diversity of sects, their beliefs and their organisational structure, Wilson (1961) developed a typology of sects to help to distinguish different types:
- Conversionist — sects that try to change the world, such as The Salvation Army.
- Adventist — sects that are awaiting some kind of divine intervention, usually the 'Second Coming' of the Messiah, for example Jehovah's Witnesses.
- Introversionist — sects that withdraw, and often live apart from the wider society in order to develop members' 'inner spirituality', such as the Amish.

Denominations

Denominations are often said to fall somewhere between a church and a sect. Some denominations, for example Methodists, developed from sects. However, this is not an inevitable process. Examples of denominations include Pentecostalists and Baptists.
- Denominations have overcome one of the problems faced by some sects, particularly those led by a charismatic leader, namely how to ensure the survival of the group after the death of the leader. Denominations have developed a more formal set of rules to ensure succession and also a hierarchical structure.
- Denominations are usually tolerant of the wider society and accept a lower level of commitment from members than do most sects.
- Members of denominations want their children to be brought up in the faith. This has led some of them to adopt the practice of infant baptism, a feature which makes denominations more like a church.

Exam tip

That the classification of religious groups was based on the Christian religion and that it is not always helpful to apply it to other religions is an important point that could gain marks for analysis and evaluation.

Knowledge check 33

Briefly explain what is meant by a 'charismatic leader'.

- Unlike sects and churches, denominations take a non-universalist approach to salvation — that is, they accept that there are other ways to salvation than through membership of their organisation.

Cults

Cults tend to be the least formally structured form of religious group. Many of them started as a private form of religion, often with a mystical dimension. It is not always necessary to 'join' the cult in any formal sense — one may simply accept the ideas and teachings of the leader. Cults do not usually have any previous ties with a religious group.

- Cults are loose-knit, non-hierarchical organisations that involve varying levels of commitment.
- Cults may appeal more to middle-class people who are seeking greater personal fulfilment or success or perhaps some spirituality in their lives.
- They often, though not always, involve payment, for example yoga classes.
- They do not necessarily involve attendance and often rely upon the use of modern technology such as the internet.

Note that a 'cult' in sociological terms does not carry the same meaning as in everyday use. In sociological terms, a cult frequently refers to a New Age movement which focuses on individual fulfilment or personal spiritual growth and often borrows ideas from ancient belief systems. Examples include yoga, feng shui and crystals.

> **Exam tip**
>
> Be aware that religious organisations reflect the values and ideas of the times in which they emerged. Also be aware that many religious organisations do not remain the same over time but evolve and change, possibly into new forms of religious organisations.

Key concepts

ideal types; church; denomination; sect; cult

Evaluation

- + Identifies key characteristics of religious organisations, showing similarities and differences between them.
- + Attempts to locate religious organisations in their historical context.
- + Shows how some religious organisations may develop over time.
- – Not always easy or possible to take account of the dynamics of groups and how they have changed over time.
- – Often very difficult to locate a religious group in a particular category.
- – Not all sects are led by a charismatic leader, and not all sects have a particularly strong appeal to members of the working class.

New religious movements

New religious movements (NRMs) is a term adopted to describe the proliferation of new religious groups throughout the world following the Second World War, and is thought to be a useful way of classifying this wide range of religious groups. Barker (2011) defines an NRM as 'a movement that has a membership consisting primarily of converts'.

The very fact that the term covers such a wide variety of groups makes classifications of NRMs difficult, but attempts have been made. Wallis (1984) developed one of the most frequently used typologies of NRMs. It was based on the group's relationship to the wider society. He concluded that NRMs could be placed into one of three main categories:

> **Exam tip**
>
> It is important to show that you recognise the considerable variety of religious movements that have been placed under the banner of NRMs.

- World-affirming — such groups accept the goals and values of the wider society, and offer members ways of achieving personal success. They are unlike many religious movements in that there is usually no theology or ritual, and members live 'normal' lives within society, attending meetings or gatherings when required or desired. An example is Transcendental Meditation (TM).
- World-accommodating — this kind of group is often an offshoot of an established church. Typically, they neither reject nor embrace the world, but work towards restoring the spiritual purity they consider the main body of the church to have lost. They sometimes believe that members have special gifts, such as prophecy or glossolalia (the ability to 'speak in tongues'). An example is the New Pentecostalists.
- World-rejecting — these groups completely reject the world around them, believing it to be evil and corrupt. They expect followers to withdraw from wider society, to a greater or lesser degree, and some of them have authoritarian regimes. Examples are the People's Temple, the Unification Church ('Moonies') and Branch Davidian.

Barker (2011) suggests that most NRMs share the following characteristics:

- As their members are converts, they tend to be more enthusiastic and active than those born into a religion.
- They are likely to appeal to an atypical sample of the population — usually younger and often from a middle-class background.
- They are usually led by a founder accorded a charismatic status by the followers. This means that the leader is unrestricted by rules or traditions.
- Tensions are likely to arise between the group and the wider society, due to the more controversial views sometimes held by the group.
- NRMs change far more rapidly and radically than older, more established religions. Inevitably, the charismatic founders will die and the initial converts will age, and therefore the demographic composition of the movements will undergo a marked transformation.

Another aspect of NRMs is that many of them have been, or will be, relatively short-lived.

Who joins NRMs?

Stark and Bainbridge (1985) found that there were two characteristics of those who joined NRMs:

- a social grievance
- a strong interpersonal bond with the person or persons who recruited them

Cadell Last (2012) of the American Humanist Association said that later research had found additional characteristics of NRMs and their members. These were:

- pre-existing social networks (friends recruited friends, family members recruited other family members)
- the development of strong social bonds between members
- existing members engaging in intensive daily interaction with new members to keep up their commitment
- weak external social ties — few friends outside the group
- limited or no experience of, or affiliation to, another religion
- members who were 'seekers' — seeking answers to the 'big questions' in life
- members who wanted direct rewards, such as self-esteem and/or a sense of power and control

Exam tip

Your class notes and textbooks will doubtless give several examples of other ways of classifying NRMs. It is important to be able to name some, but it is unlikely that you will need to go into great detail. What is important is that you are able to show analysis and evaluation by pointing out the various problems of classifying so many diverse groups, but also the ways in which such classifications may be helpful.

Some NRMs that start by being in tension with the wider society gradually adapt; the 'them and us' characteristic declines and they become more like other, conventional, religious movements. This process is called 'denominationalisation'. It can be applied to the Society of Friends (Quakers), though it is important to stress that this process happens in relatively few movements and is by no means inevitable.

New Age movements

Unlike most formal religions, New Age movements (NAMs) have no holy text, no central organisation, no formal membership, no ordained ministers and no central body of belief. This means that the term 'New Age movements' serves as a kind of umbrella term for quite diverse groups. In many respects, NAMs reflect characteristics of the postmodern era, including a greater emphasis on individualism, consumerism and choice.

New Age movements developed in the Western world in the 1970s. They are seen as a form of alternative NRM, with a focus on such diverse concerns as inner spirituality, the environment, spiritualism, mysticism, astrology, paganism and magic. Their beliefs and practices are so diverse that some have argued that it is difficult to think of them in terms of a 'movement' at all. While many people hold some beliefs that might be termed 'New Age' ones, such as a belief in the importance of protecting the environment or a belief in alternative forms of healing, actual membership of New Age groups is small.

Bruce (1991) sees such groups as characterised by 'eclecticism', meaning that they bring together a variety of beliefs. However, they almost all have a focus on the 'inner self' and the belief that there is a need to turn inwards to retrieve and develop 'inner wisdom'. Many NAMs are characterised by their commercialism and there is a healthy market in books, magazines, crystals and other items with 'healing properties' or the alleged ability to work magic.

Knowledge check 34

Why might someone with weak external ties be attracted to an NRM?

Exam tip

If a question asks about NAMs, show that you know that the term covers a wide variety of groups.

Key concepts

new religious movements; world-affirming; world-accommodating; world-rejecting; New Age movements; eclecticism

Evaluation

- + NRMs, as a wider term than sects or cults, are a more appropriate way of defining the many new religious groups that have developed since the latter part of the twentieth century.
- + NRMs have met a religious or spiritual need for some who might not have engaged with mainstream religions.
- + Some NRMs have caused mainstream religions to reflect on their basic values and the extent to which these are still reflected in their beliefs and practices.
- − The terms NRMs and NAMs cover such a wide variation of movements that it is often difficult to fit some groups into a particular classification.
- − Some NRMs have caused public concerns over their controlling tendencies, particularly those in which members have harmed themselves or others.
- − Not all NRMs have a particular appeal to the working class, nor do all members join out of a sense of deprivation.

Summary

- There are various ways of classifying religious organisations.
- While classifications are helpful, they are ideal types, and many organisations and groups do not fit easily into classifications.
- Most religious organisations experience greater or lesser changes over time, so may fit more easily into a classification at one stage of their development than another.
- Some groups are secretive and/or hostile to outsiders, so knowledge of these may be partial.
- Most classifications apply only to Christian groups and it is difficult and often unwise to apply them to other religions.
- There has been a growth in both NRMs and NAMs since the mid-twentieth century.

Religious/spiritual organisations and social groups

The latest census, in 2011, asked people about their religion. The question was voluntary, but only 7% did not answer. For England and Wales, these were the replies given:

- Christian   59%
- Muslim   5%
- Other   4%
- Not stated   7%
- No religion   25%

These figures show that almost six out of ten people in England and Wales describe their religion as Christian. However, comparison with the 2001 census shows the following:

- The proportion stating that they had 'no religion' rose from 14.8% to 25.1%.
- The proportion stating that they were Christian fell from 71.7% to 59.3%.
- All 'other' religions increased — the largest increase being among Muslims, from 3.0% to 4.8%.

Religion and social class

Historically in Britain there was a fairly close relationship between social class and religious participation. In the postmodern world this relationship has fragmented, and a number of researchers and social surveys have found that social class is less important than other factors such as age, ethnicity and gender as indicators of both religious belief and practice.

For Marx, religion was a human creation and ideological, and was an instrument of the bourgeoisie used to confirm the right of the rich to their wealth and privilege and to persuade the working class to accept their inferior position in society.

Weber introduced the concept of the **ideology of disprivilege** to explain the attraction of certain sects to the working class, as they taught that earthly sufferings were a test of faith, and that the poor would receive salvation and rewards in the afterlife.

Ideology of disprivilege Refers to religious explanations which legitimise earthly inequalities. The variant term 'theodicy of disprivilege' is also found.

World-affirming groups such as Scientology and the Alpha Course, with their promise of how to achieve worldly success, have a particular appeal to the middle classes. Similarly, many Christian evangelical sects draw their membership primarily from the poorer sections of society. Steve Bruce also points out that New Age movements have a primarily middle-class (and female) membership, as only the relatively well-off can afford the time and money to devote to their practices.

The *British Social Attitudes* (BSA) survey of 2012 found that the group of people who never attended religious services included similar proportions of people from different socioeconomic classes. Using the NS-SEC classification, the survey found that 63.3% of the salariat (salaried white-collar workers) said that they never attended a religious service, while the figure rose to 67.9% of the working class.

However, an online YouGov poll conducted in September 2014, covering 7,212 adults aged 16-plus, found that of those who *were* regular attenders at religious services, 63% were middle class (ABC1) and 38% were working class (C2DE).

Religion and gender

Much research has shown that on almost all indicators of religiosity, women are more 'religious' than men. That is, they are more likely than men to believe in God and life after death, attend religious services, pray and read the Bible regularly. On average, 65% of the members of congregations at UK churches are women.

A report published in 2015 with findings from the 1970 *British Cohort Study* based on 9,000 people showed that 34% of women were self-reported atheists or agnostics compared with 54% of men, and 36% of women said that they did not believe in life after death compared with 63% of men. Data from the *British Social Attitudes* survey of 2017 show that religious participation continues to be gendered. In every age category, men were less likely than women to say that they had a religion, went to church or believed in God; 41% of all men claimed to have a religion compared with 54% of women.

Several explanations have been put forward for such gender differences in religiosity.

- Traditionally, mothers have the major role in child-rearing, and see church-going and church activities as part of their role of instilling moral values in their children.
- When many women did not work outside the home, they had more time for church-going during the week.
- There are different patterns of socialisation for males and females, with males socialised to be more aggressive and rational, while females are encouraged to develop their emotional side, making them more receptive to issues of morality.
- Until recently, men and women operated in very different spheres — the socially gendered division of labour led to their having different structural locations, with men more exposed to the wider society through their work and women more confined to the domestic sphere. Men were thus more likely to pick up new ideas and attitudes, such as those concerned with growing secularisation.

In the Western world, according to Hoffman (2018), females are more likely than males to be involved in a variety of religious practices and to report stronger religious beliefs, levels of commitment, and spirituality. Hoffman argues that there are many reasons for this, including class position, gender roles and the division of labour,

Exam tip

When quoting findings from social surveys, show that you are aware that the different methods of survey data collection each have their weaknesses.

Knowledge check 35

State two potential disadvantages of online surveys.

Exam tip

As with all explanations of social phenomena, you should be able to discuss any problems or weaknesses in the arguments. If you look at the list on the left, you should be able to find some criticisms that could be made of them.

amount of free time, social and cultural power and authority, control over sexuality and different rates of secularisation. However, a significant finding was that women are less likely to take risks and engage with behaviour that deviates from what is expected.

Another reason for women appearing to be more religious is the 'feminisation' of the church that has occurred. Women increasingly play important leadership roles. The first women priests in the Church of England were ordained in 1994. Women can now become bishops. In the Church of England, the first ordination of a woman into the priesthood was in 1994 and the first consecration of a woman as bishop was in 2015.

However, most of the literature about the gendered nature of religion relates to Western Christianity. A closer look at other religions shows that among Jews, Muslims and Hindus, men are more religious than women, at least in terms of their attendance at services of worship. This casts doubt on the assumption that women are inherently more religious than men, and draws attention to social and cultural factors.

Religion and age

Age is one of the most important social factors associated with religiosity. In the UK, according to Bullivant (2017), only 7% of young adults identify as Anglican, which is less than the 10% who categorise themselves as Catholic. Young Muslims, at 6%, are close to overtaking those who consider themselves part of the country's established church.

Bullivant carried out comparative research across Europe and found that many young Europeans were baptised, but are unlikely to ever set foot inside a church. This suggests that cultural religious identities are not being passed on from parents to children.

Bullivant's figures for the UK were partly explained by high immigration: for example, one in five Catholics in the UK were not born in the UK. Furthermore, the Muslim birth rate is higher than that of the general population, and the Muslim community has much higher numbers of people who retain their religious identity.

The 2011 census replies showed that the highest proportions of self-reported Christians were in the 45–69 age group. With regard to the mainstream Christian churches, it seems likely that the fall in both members and congregations will continue as older members and worshippers die and do not seem likely to be replaced by younger people. Evangelical churches might fare better, as they seem to appeal to younger members. It is also likely that Muslim congregations will not decline as rapidly as some other groups, as in many cases their religion is an essential part of their ethnic identity.

Reasons given for the age profile of the main Christian churches include that their older members grew up in a more 'religious' age than at present, where Sunday school and church attendance were far more prevalent than today. Those born and growing up in a more secular age seem less likely to identify with, and practise, a religious faith, with the probable exception of those in evangelical churches and from black and minority ethnic (BAME) backgrounds.

Exam tip

It is important to be able to make at least brief comparisons between different religions when discussing gender and religiosity. In particular, the role of women in Islam varies considerably between societies.

Knowledge check 36

Why might evangelical churches, whose membership is drawn primarily from black and immigrant groups, have a different age profile from Anglican congregations?

Exam tip

While you will not be expected to remember exact percentages in an exam, it is helpful to show a rough idea of proportions.

Eileen Barker (2011) looked at how several NRMs that emerged around the 1970s were coping with an ageing membership. She points out that there are two main ways for an organisation to preserve a younger age profile. One is the birth of a second or even third generation, as the original members have families, and the other is by the recruitment of younger members.

With regard to the first, several NRMs (e.g. the Children of God and the Unification Church) found that children born into the movement left as soon as possible, so this is a far from reliable way of keeping a movement going.

With regard to the second, converts, which is what most members of NRMs are, have a tendency to attract and recruit people of their own age. This explains the young age profile of new movements, but also means that as the original members age, so do new converts. Barker concludes that this process will result in some movements possibly dying out by the end of the century. Many movements, particularly **millenarian** ones, have made no provision for looking after ageing members, and the members have made no provision for themselves, as a result of their lifestyle within the movement.

Barker comes to the conclusion that the longer a religious movement has been in existence, the more likely it is to have faced the problems of an ageing membership and to have developed strategies to deal with the issue.

Religion and ethnicity

The term 'ethnic' is usually used to define or describe a group of people sharing a common cultural heritage. Religion is an important component of any cultural heritage, but it is more important to some groups than to others, or more important at one period than another.

In general, minority ethnic groups in the UK have higher rates of religious participation and affiliation. According to Bullivant (2017), people who claim no religion are more likely to be white than non-white. Part of the reason for this pattern is that minority ethnic groups, such as Muslims, tend to have a younger age profile and higher fertility rates, and therefore these groups are growing. Another interesting recent finding was that the Church of England tends to be dominated by white British people, while alternative, more contemporary religious groups tend to appeal more to minority ethnic groups.

One important question has been what happens to both religious and ethnic identities with regard to second- and third-generation immigrants. Nandi and Platt (2018) carried out a survey in which they discovered that Muslims are often perceived to have a stronger ethnic identity. However, they state that this is particularly true of second-generation Muslims in the UK. Furthermore, they found that ethnic identity is also tied to political identity.

Bruce (2002) argues that some minority ethnic groups find religion important in two particular ways:

- *Cultural transition*: as minority ethnic groups move into a new area, religion is useful as a support mechanism to help settle in and build community networks.
- *Cultural defence*: some minority ethnic groups use religion as a way to protect their identity, for instance to seek refuge from hostility or prejudice (e.g. in response to Islamophobia).

Millenarian movement
One that believes that there will be a significant event, usually the Second Coming of Christ, that will change the world order and lead to 1,000 years of blessedness. The event that will trigger this is often thought to be imminent, and the members believe they will be among the 'saved'.

Exam tip

Being able to state that religious identity is, for many British-born members of minority ethnic groups, more important than ethnic identity, and also to show that there are differences between different groups, would gain you important marks for both analysis and evaluation.

Knowledge check 37

Give two reasons why minority ethnic groups may be more religious than the ethnic majority.

Key concepts

social class; ethnicity; ideology of disprivilege; social spheres; gendered religion; millenarianism; cultural transition; cultural defence

Evaluation

- ■ + It is useful to examine the composition of religious groups with reference to class, gender, age and ethnicity.
- ■ + The Marxist concept of ideology and the Weberian concept of the ideology of disprivilege are helpful in analysing the links between religion and social class.
- ■ + Age is one of the most important social factors associated with different levels of religiosity.
- ■ + Research shows the importance of religious identity to many minority ethnic groups.
- ■ + It is important to look at how religious beliefs and practice might differ between first-generation immigrants and subsequent generations.
- ■ − The relationship between religion and social class is less pronounced than it used to be.
- ■ − Some of the explanations of the apparently greater religiosity of women are outdated in terms of women's roles.

Summary

- ■ Membership of religious groups and organisations varies by social class, gender, age and ethnicity.
- ■ Particularly in the Christian church, age appears to be the most important factor in explaining different levels of religiosity.
- ■ Many NRMs, especially millenarian movements, are facing difficulties in dealing with an ageing membership.

- ■ Religious identity is very important to many members of minority ethnic groups, usually more important than ethnic identity.
- ■ There are variations, sometimes significant, both between and within religious organisations.

■ The significance of religion and religiosity in the contemporary world

This topic includes discussion of the nature and extent of secularisation in a global context and of globalisation and the spread of religions. While the main focus of this topic is the UK, it is important to be able to place sociological discussions of religion and religiosity in a global context. Many of the issues facing the world are linked, to a greater or lesser extent, with religious ideologies. In the UK, undoubtedly now a multi-faith society, people on a daily basis come into contact with those holding diverse religious beliefs and, increasingly, with those of no religious beliefs.

In some parts of the world people of different religions and no religion live and work alongside each other in relative harmony, while in other places people are persecuted for belonging to a particular religion. Religion is inextricably linked to politics and political action, sometimes with violent consequences. Whatever a person's beliefs, religion is something that cannot be ignored.

Exam tip

Make sure in any discussion of secularisation that you make clear which definition(s) you are using.

The nature and extent of secularisation

Secularisation: the concept

Secularisation is one of the most complex sociological concepts, and has been defined in many different ways.

Secularisation and the 'founding fathers'

Comte, Marx, Durkheim and Weber all argued that some degree of secularisation would be an inevitable outcome of **modernity**. Berger (1974) defined modernity as 'the growth and diffusion of a set of institutions rooted in the transformation of the economy by means of technology'.

- Comte believed that as societies developed from the theological to the positivist stage, social behaviour would be directed by scientific, rational thought. As sociologists understood society, Comte believed that they would be able to bring about a new moral order based on scientific understanding, and sociology would become the new, secular, religion.
- Marx believed that after the proletarian revolution there would be no need for religion, as the conditions that created religion, i.e. the existence of capitalism and the bourgeoisie, would disappear. In the new communist society there would be no need for people to seek comfort in the belief of a better life in the hereafter.
- Durkheim also saw the role of religion changing as societies became more complex, with social cohesion coming to be achieved by laws of contract rather than the shared norms and values arising out of religious beliefs and rituals.
- Weber believed that the increasing rationality of complex industrial societies would lead to greater bureaucracy and centralised control, and there would be little room for belief in supernatural forces. He described this as 'the disenchantment' of the world.

Modernity In Europe usually refers to the period from the Enlightenment of the eighteenth century to the mid-twentieth century. It is where there is a decline in tradition and the development of a rational outlook on social issues, together with an attempt to shape social arrangements according to logical and scientific principles.

The meaning of secularisation
Bryan Wilson

A commonly used definition is that of Wilson (1966), which is that secularisation is the process whereby religious thinking, practice and organisations lose their social significance. This definition has four parts. First, it describes a process, so this is something that takes place over time. This process then has three elements to it — thinking, practice and organisations. To explore the nature and extent of secularisation, then, we would have to look at each of these elements. Religious thinking and practice have sometimes been referred to as the 'three Bs' — believing, behaving and belonging. The final element is that of religious organisations — again, made complex by the increasing variety of religious groups in society.

Exam tip

If appropriate, it is useful to be able to refer to the fact that ideas about the decline of religion existed in the work of the 'founding fathers'. Their reasons and predictions differed, but they all predicted a decline in the importance of religion in the modern world.

Another, and important, aspect of secularisation is to note exactly where we are looking. Many discussions are highly ethnocentric — they focus almost exclusively on Christianity, and on the Western world.

Steve Bruce

For Bruce, secularisation is 'a long-term decline in the power, popularity and prestige of religious beliefs and rituals', which he claims is brought about by 'individualism, diversity and egalitarianism in the context of liberal democracy'.

Evaluation

- ■ + Without the concept of secularisation, it would be difficult to analyse and explain the undoubted changes that are taking place in religious belief and activity.
- ■ + It is important to have clear definitions of secularisation because they determine how sociologists measure its nature and extent.
- ■ − The plurality of definitions makes it difficult to compare different accounts of the nature and extent of secularisation.
- ■ − Many discourses on secularisation are ethnocentric, looking only at Christianity in Western, developed societies.

Secularisation: believing

While one way of gauging the extent of people's belief is by what they do, such as how often they attend religious services, the most usual way, at least as far as the UK is concerned, is by looking at what they say. A number of surveys have looked at the extent to which people, regardless of their religious affiliation or practices, say that they believe in God, or a god, or a higher spiritual power. All surveys show a decline in the proportion of UK adults who say that they have such a belief.

A YouGov survey in 2015 found that a third (33%) of adults say they do not believe in God or a greater spiritual power of any kind. This is very similar to the proportion (32%) who said that they believed in 'a god'. A fifth (20%) said that they believed in 'a higher power', but not a god, while 14% said they did not know what they believed.

As seen earlier, belief, or lack of it, varies with age. In the YouGov poll, only 25% of 18- to 24-year-olds believed in God or a higher spiritual power, while 40% had no belief at all in a god or higher spiritual power. Conversely, 41% of over-60s believed in God. The same poll showed that only 55% of those self-identifying as Christian actually believed in God, while 23% believed in 'some sort of greater spiritual power', though not a god, while 9% of self-identifying Christians said they didn't believe in any higher power. David Voas (2003) is sceptical of the data relating to those who state that they have a belief in God, saying that such professed beliefs were rarely acted upon.

Key concepts

belief; God; higher spiritual power; atheist; agnostic

Knowledge check 38

Briefly explain the difference between an atheist and an agnostic.

Exam tip

It is always useful to be able to refer to findings from different religions.

Evaluation

- ▪ + There is evidence that there is a declining belief in God or some other spiritual power.
- ▪ + The decline in belief appears stronger among younger people.
- ▪ − Following trends over time is difficult as survey questions are not all the same.
- ▪ − We have to take note of possible differences between people of different religions.
- ▪ − Some people may claim a belief in God or a spiritual power without this having any impact on their life.

Secularisation: behaving

By 'behaving', we are talking about religious practice — attending religious services, praying, following religious rules governing diet or dress, and so on. Some of the evidence is from quantitative data, such as church attendance statistics, but much is qualitative and based on what people say that they do.

Attendance at worship

To put church attendance in context, in 1851 about half of the population in Britain attended church regularly. The figure is now around 5%. According to the Church of England, the number of people attending their Sunday services fell in 2018 to 722,000 — 18,000 fewer than in 2016 — continuing a trend seen over recent decades. In the UK, England had the lowest percentage of the population attending church in 2015 (4.7%), just below Wales at 4.8%. In Scotland, the equivalent figure is 8.9% (Brierley Consultancy 2017). However, according to the Pew Forum (2017), 20% of the UK population say they attend religious services at least monthly.

One problem with survey data on this topic is that research has shown that people tend to exaggerate, or fail to recall accurately, how often they have attended religious services for purposes other than weddings, baptisms or funerals.

The Roman Catholic Church in the UK has had its congregations significantly boosted in some areas by the influx of devout young people from eastern Europe. Overall, however, the Roman Catholic Church shows a similar pattern to many other churches and large denominations. One group of UK churches not following the trend of falling congregations are denominational forms of Christianity, whose congregations are largely people of Afro-Caribbean and African descent. Such churches are attracting ever-growing congregations, and it has been estimated that there are over half a million committed black Christians in the UK who attend worship on a frequent and regular basis. Most black churches are **Pentecostal** in nature.

Key concepts

church attendance; black churches; Pentecostal; mega-church; evangelical

Knowledge check 39

Why might measuring religiosity through 'behaving' be better than measuring it through 'believing'?

Pentecostalism A form of Christianity that emphasises the work of the Holy Spirit and believes that members should have direct experience of the presence of God. Services are energetic and dynamic, often with a strong focus on music and singing. Other features are 'speaking in tongues', faith healing and prophesying.

Exam tip

You will always be rewarded for showing that you recognise differences between various religious groups.

Evaluation

- ■ + The data appear consistent in showing that there has been a decline in many examples of religious behaviour, particularly attending services of worship.
- ■ + There are important differences between different branches of religion.
- ■ + The arrival of immigrants has had an impact on both traditional and newer forms of Christian worship.
- ■ − Particularly with some of the black evangelical churches, which may start as relatively informal groups meeting in people's homes, it is difficult to obtain figures for the number of worshippers.
- ■ − All data must be treated with caution, as there are significant possibilities of error.

Secularisation: belonging

In this context, 'belonging' refers to people's membership of various religious groups. This is a particularly difficult area for which to obtain even reasonably accurate statistics, particularly where membership of smaller groups, NRMs and New Age groups are concerned.

In addition, some churches cannot or do not collect membership statistics. As far as Christian churches are concerned, the Roman Catholic Church does not have 'members' — people are either 'part of the Catholic population' or 'Mass attenders'. The first gives an unrealistic view, so the usual measure of 'belonging' here is the number of people who attend Mass. Most new churches and virtually all Pentecostal groups count attendance only rather than any formal 'membership'. The Church of England uses the figures from its electoral roll, which are invariably higher than attendance numbers. Presbyterians, meanwhile, apply the notion of membership rigorously and can supply detailed figures. Baptist and Methodist membership figures are available from their head offices. The Salvation Army, Lutheran churches and Quakers can provide membership information, but the many overseas national churches, such as the Nigerian Redeemed Christian Church of God, have no membership figures and so provide attendance data only. Information about 'membership', then, can give only a very broad picture.

Looking at data on membership of UK churches from 1900, the peak year in terms of members was 1930, when there were 10.9 million members.

Peter Brierley (2018), an expert on church statistics, states that in the UK Anglican churches are in major decline, while new forms of church such as Pentecostal churches are growing. Not all forms of denomination are growing; Brierley points out that Methodist churches are in decline.

In summary, then, the 'belonging' aspect of secularisation indicates that membership of established churches and denominations is falling, while there is considerable growth in membership of evangelical and Pentecostal churches, particularly those with primarily Afro-Caribbean and African congregations.

Key concepts

membership; attendance

Knowledge check 40

Identify and briefly explain two reasons why it might be difficult to get membership figures for New Age groups.

Exam tip

Even if you don't quote the actual examples of which groups can and cannot provide membership details, being able to explain the problems of gathering accurate data is important and will help to gain marks for evaluation.

Evaluation

- + Membership/attendance figures indicate that secularisation is occurring, at least as far as the Christian faith is concerned.
- + The process is not, however, universal — some types of religious organisation are significantly increasing their membership, albeit from a relatively small base.
- – The figures need to be treated with caution, as it is difficult to obtain accurate data.
- – The data cover only larger and only Christian denominations — there are no accurate figures for membership of smaller and New Age groups, though these are likely to be very small.

Secularisation: religious organisations

The *British Social Attitudes* survey of 2017 identified three key trends:

- the continued rise in the number of religious 'nones'
- the sharp decline in Christianity, and within that religion the huge shift away from mainstream denominations to evangelical and Pentecostal churches
- the increased diversity of religion and the rapid growth of the Muslim, Sikh and Hindu populations in the UK

Knowledge check 41

What is meant by 'humanism'?

Secularisation in the USA

Traditionally the USA has been perceived to be more religious in terms of all measures, but in the past decade there have been some significant changes. According to the Public Religion Research Institute (2017), the religious landscape is more diverse today than at any time since modern sociological measurements began.

- White Christians, who still dominated the religious landscape as recently as a decade ago, now account for fewer than half of the public. White evangelical Protestants, the single largest religious tradition, make up less than one in five Americans today (17%).
- Compared to ten years ago, significantly fewer Americans identify as white mainline (i.e. mainstream) Protestant (13%) or white Catholic (11%).
- Fifteen percent of Americans are non-white Protestants, including black Protestants (8%), Hispanic Protestants (4%), and Asian, mixed-race and other race Protestants (3%). Seven percent of the public is Hispanic Catholic.
- Non-Christian religious groups make up less than one in ten Americans. Muslims, Buddhists and Hindus are each around 1% of the population, while Jewish Americans account for 2%.
- Nearly one in four Americans (24%) are now religiously unaffiliated. No religious group is larger than that group.
- Age is significant. Nearly two thirds of people aged 65 or older identify as white and Christian: white evangelical Protestant (26%), white mainline Protestant (19%) or white Catholic (16%). In contrast, only about one quarter of young adults (age 18–29) belong to a white Christian tradition, including white evangelical Protestant (8%), white mainline Protestant (8%) or white Catholic (6%). Young adults are more than three times as likely as seniors to identify as religiously unaffiliated (38% vs 12%, respectively).

Exam tip

There are lots of figures here, which are included to indicate to you the scale of what is happening. You are not expected to remember all the various percentages, but you do need to know what they indicate in terms of an overall situation or trend.

Thus, the overall picture from the USA shows that while levels of religiosity are considerably higher than in most European countries, the trend indicates that secularisation is beginning to occur. As younger Americans are less religious than their elders, it can be assumed that the process will continue.

Why is the USA different?

Both Wilson (1996) and Bruce (2013) put forward interesting hypotheses to explain the differences between religion in the USA and Europe. Wilson said that while Europeans secularised by abandoning their churches, Americans secularised their religion. Bruce's version of this idea was that secularisation has taken two forms: 'In Europe the churches became less popular; in the United States the churches became less religious.'

- Religion in the USA has become less about salvation and worship and more about personal fulfilment.
- US churches have also embraced many secular activities, developing their own radio and television stations and turning their churches more into community centres, running schools, play groups, therapy groups, gyms and so on.
- Bruce suggests that 'the purpose of religion is no longer to glorify God; it is to help find peace of mind and personal satisfaction'.

Knowledge check 42

Briefly explain why the concept of 'secularisation' might not mean the same thing when applied to European and US populations.

Key concepts

secularisation; religious affiliation; religiosity; traditional values

Evaluation

- + Levels of belief and religiosity in the USA continue to be much higher than in European countries, casting some doubt on the secularisation thesis.
- − Despite this, the trend suggests that Americans are becoming less religious in terms of believing, belonging and behaving.
- − Many American churches and groups have adopted more secular ideas and patterns of behaviour, suggesting that in the USA, religion itself is becoming secular.

Globalisation and the spread of religions

The global picture

Globally, 84% of the population claims an affiliation to a religion (The Pew Centre 2015). By contrast, the UK is one of the least religious countries in the world. In a global ranking of 65 countries in 2015, the UK came six places from the bottom, with only 30% of the population saying that they were religious. This compares with 94% of people in Thailand and 93% of people in Armenia, Bangladesh, Georgia and Morocco. At the bottom of the list were China (6%), Japan (13%) and Sweden (19%). Research into religion worldwide in 2015 showed that poorer nations tend to be more religious than wealthier nations. This is in part due to the fact that people turn to religion when their lives feel insecure.

Knowledge check 43

Give one reason for the very low figure of those claiming to be religious in China.

Global trend 1: traditional religion is growing

While traditional Christianity is declining in membership in the UK, non-traditional religions are seeing an increase both in the UK and elsewhere. However, not all traditional religions are experiencing a similar level of decline.

■ Islam is actually growing globally, which is reflected in membership figures. This is partly due to demographic trends: Muslims on average are younger and have significantly higher fertility rates. The Pew Centre (2017) predicts that globally, babies born to Muslims will begin to outnumber Christian births by 2035; on the other hand, there will be a sharp decrease in the fertility rates of people with no religion. By 2055 to 2060, just 9% of all babies will be born to religiously unaffiliated women, while 71% will be born to either Muslims (36%) or Christians (35%).

■ Hinduism is also increasing. It is the fastest growing religion in Pakistan and Saudi Arabia. The Pew Report (2015) again links this increase to fertility, particularly in Pakistan.

Global trend 2: growth in membership of Christian denominations

There has been a significant increase in denominations, particularly Christian denominations. In 1900, there were less than 1 million Pentecostals/Charismatics in the world. In 2017, they will climb to 669 million. By 2050, they will top 1 billion — the second Christian group to do so, behind Catholics.

■ The growth is seen particularly in places such as Nigeria, where rapid social change has led to people wishing to turn to a form of religion that they can relate to, that provides security and identity in times of uncertainty.

■ Evangelicals and Pentecostalism are growing much faster than traditional Christianity globally, particularly in Latin America. While initially the growth of Pentecostalism was seen largely among poor people, it is now spreading to middle-class professionals, who find appeal in the emphasis on 'inner healing', individual responsibility and prosperity. A further group joining the converts are men who are struggling with alcohol and substance abuse. The Pentecostalist teachings promote a healthy lifestyle and offer help to those with addictions.

Religion and globalisation

The relationship between religion and globalisation is a complex one. One effect of globalisation is that ideas and information spread rapidly around the globe. It is thus easier for people to know about other cultures, including their religions. The growth of global political forums and transnational corporations has had an effect on religious organisations, many of which are now international with a global reach. Religious organisations have also benefited from the spread of global technologies, with developments such as websites and online sales of tracts and merchandise. Another effect of globalisation has been the growth of insecurity and mental stress, and many people have found hope and comfort in religion.

Negative effects have been seen in the rise of religious-based terrorism spreading beyond the country of origin, with groups such as Boko Haram waging war in the name of their faith.

Knowledge check 44

Why might denominational forms of religion appeal more than traditional forms of religion?

Exam tip

Discussion of the decline in Catholicism and the growth of Pentecostalism in Latin America will enable you to show that there are differences within the broader Christian faith, which will help gain marks for analysis and evaluation in a debate about secularisation.

Secularisation: the global context

In the world as a whole, there are two distinct processes going on. In the majority of Western countries, there is considerable evidence that on almost all indices, people are becoming less religious, and one could say with confidence that there is a strong case in favour of secularisation. Even regarding the USA, which is often given as an example against secularisation, many have pointed to the ways in which religion itself has taken on many secular features.

In many other parts of the world, however, religion is thriving and the case for secularisation is weak. In the late 1980s, Peter Berger, once a staunch believer in secularisation, said that he no longer believed in the secularisation thesis, as it could not explain the growth of radical Islam, fundamental and Pentecostal Christianity in Asia, Africa and Latin America, or the significant growth of evangelical mega-churches in the USA. These concerns were also shared by Rodney Stark.

Key concepts

projected changes; Latin American Pentecostalism; Islam; demography

Evaluation

- ■ + With the exception of the USA, there is a link between levels of wealth or poverty and the extent of secularisation.
- ■ + It is predicted that almost all of the world's major religions will grow over the next 40 years.
- ■ + Pentecostalist Christianity has shown strong growth in Latin America.
- ■ + Islam in particular is predicted to show strong growth.
- ■ + Some of the negative effects of globalisation on people's lives may increase the degree of religiosity.
- ■ − The apparent greater religiosity of the USA may mask a process of secularisation both within and outside the churches.
- ■ − The growth of Islam will be a result of demographic factors rather than more people converting to the faith.
- ■ − Political events may serve to increase tensions between Muslim and non-Muslim populations in Europe.

> **Exam tip**
>
> When writing about secularisation, it is very important that you are clear about which parts of the world you are referring to. Being able to discuss the contrast between Europe and some other parts of the world will allow you to show the skills of analysis and evaluation. However, the focus of the question is likely to be on the UK and Europe, so keep your answer in proportion.

Summary

- ■ When discussing secularisation, it is important to know which definition is being used.
- ■ There is considerable evidence in Western countries that levels of religiosity are declining, particularly among younger people.
- ■ In the UK, despite evidence that overall levels of secularisation are rising, some churches, particularly evangelical and Pentecostal groups with largely black membership, are growing.

- ■ The USA appears to differ from other Western countries in that the population shows much higher levels of religiosity, but even here, there is evidence of a process of secularisation.
- ■ Globally, religion remains very important to a high percentage of the world's population, with poorer countries showing much higher levels of religiosity than wealthier ones.
- ■ Islam is the only world religion predicted to grow at a faster rate than the world's population over the next 40 years.

Questions & Answers

How to use this section

In this section you will find two sets of exam-style questions. Each set comprises three questions for each section, i.e. three for *Families and households* and three for *Beliefs in society*. These are laid out as you will find them in Paper 2 of your exam.

Each question is followed by a brief analysis of what to watch out for when answering it. Each question has two student answers, one at about an A grade (Student A) and the other at about a C grade (Student B), with comments on the answers throughout.

Remember that there is no single perfect way of answering an exam question — the highest marks can be gained by taking different approaches, especially in the higher-mark questions. However, the comments should help to show you the kinds of approach that would do well and some of the pitfalls to avoid.

As a general point, you should always read through the whole question before starting to write. When you come to answer the question that is based on an 'item', read the item particularly carefully, as it will contain material that is essential to answering the question.

Examinable skills

AQA sociology examination papers are designed to test certain defined skills. These skills are expressed as assessment objectives (AOs). There are three AOs and it is important that you know what these are and what you have to be able to do in an exam to show your ability in each. Further guidance on each of the AOs is given in the comments on the sample questions and answers. In practice, many answers to questions, particularly those carrying the higher marks, will contain elements of all three AOs.

Assessment objective 1

Demonstrate knowledge and understanding of:
- **sociological theories, concepts and evidence**
- **sociological research methods**

Your exam answers will have to demonstrate clearly to the examiners that your knowledge is accurate and appropriate to the topic being discussed and that you have a clear understanding. It is not enough simply to reproduce knowledge learned by rote; you must be able to use this knowledge in a meaningful way to answer the specific question set. This means that you must be able to *select* the appropriate knowledge from everything you know and use only the knowledge that is relevant to, and addresses the issues raised by, the question.

Assessment objective 2

Apply sociological theories, concepts, evidence and research methods to a range of issues.

In certain questions in the exam you will be presented with an 'item' — a short paragraph setting the context for the question that is to follow and providing you with some information to help answer it. You *must* take this relevant information and use (apply) it in your answer. However, 'applying' the material does not mean simply copying it from the item and leaving it to speak for itself. You will need to show your understanding of the material by doing something with it, such as offering a criticism, explaining something about it, linking it to a particular sociological theory or offering another example of what is being stated or suggested. You will therefore be using your own knowledge to add to the information that you have been given and will be *applying* it appropriately to answer the question.

Assessment objective 3

Analyse and evaluate sociological theories, concepts, evidence and research methods in order to:
- **present arguments**
- **make judgements**
- **draw conclusions**

The skill of *analysis* is shown by breaking something down into its component parts and subjecting those parts to detailed examination. Analysis is shown by providing answers (depending, of course, on what you are analysing) to questions such as 'Who said or who believes this?', 'What does this concept relate to?', 'What does this research method entail?', 'How was this evidence collected?' and so on.

The skill of *evaluation* is shown by the ability to identify the strengths and weaknesses or limitations of any sociological material. It is not sufficient, however, simply to list the strengths or limitations of something — you need to be able to say *why* something is considered a strength or otherwise, and sometimes you will need to state *who* claims that this is a strength or weakness. Depending on what you are discussing, you may be able to reach a conclusion about the relative merits or otherwise of something, but remember that any conclusions should be based on the rational arguments and solid sociological evidence that you have presented during your answer.

Weighting of assessment objectives

In the exam papers, each AO is given a particular weighting, which indicates its relative importance to the overall mark gained.

Weighting for A-level examinations (approximate %)				
Assessment objective	Paper 1	Paper 2	Paper 3	Overall weighting
AO1	15	13	16	44
AO2	11	11	9	31
AO3	8	9	8	25
Overall	34	33	33	100

Command words

Ofqual, the body that sets the criteria for all GCE sociology specifications, has an approved list of 'command words' used in exam questions. The following are some of the most commonly used, but it is important to remember that the list is not exhaustive and occasionally other, similar words or phrases may be used instead. All this shows how important it is to take time in an exam and read the questions carefully before you start writing. It is worth learning what is meant by these command words to ensure you give an appropriate response.

- *Outline* — give the main characteristics.
- *Outline and explain* — give the main characteristics and develop these.
- *Analyse* — separate information into components and identify their characteristics.
- *Evaluate* — make judgements from the available evidence.
- *Applying material from the item ...* — draw on the material provided and develop it using your own knowledge to answer the question.

The A-level examination

The topics of *Families and households* and *Beliefs in society* are examined in Paper 2 of the A-level examination, Topics in Sociology. The *Families and households* questions appear in Section A of Paper 2, as one of four options. The *Beliefs in society* questions appear in section B, as one of four options.

The *whole* exam lasts for 2 hours, carries 80 marks and is worth one third of the A-level qualification. The *Families and households* questions make up one half of the exam and carry 40 marks; *Beliefs in society* is also worth 40 marks. You should therefore allow about an hour for answering the *Families and households* questions and an hour for answering the *Beliefs in society* questions. Allow 25–30 minutes for the last question for each topic, which carries 20 marks. Try to manage your time so that you have time to read through the whole paper at the end.

Test paper 1

Section A: Families and households

Question 1

Outline and explain two ways in which changes in the fertility rate have led to changes in structures in the family.

(10 marks)

> Be careful not to write about reasons for the decreasing fertility rate. The question is asking you about the impact of decreasing birth rates on family structures, meaning types of families.

Question 2

Item A

Recently, some sociologists have begun to explore who has control in relationships in the family. This is a complex and sensitive area of family life to research. While some sociologists have explored decision making, others have explored conflict or control of finances.

Applying material from Item A, analyse two reasons why power relations in the family remain unequal.

(10 marks)

> For 'analyse' questions you need to choose two 'hooks' from the item. Base each paragraph on one of these hooks, considering carefully what you are going to say about each before you begin writing.

Question 3

Item B

Some sociologists argue that social forces shape behaviour, for example, families socialising children into the values of society. Others however argue that this approach ignores the fact that people have free will. Some sociologists argue that we have moved into a new era of choice and this is the only way to understand family life today.

Applying material from Item B and your knowledge, evaluate the view that structural explanations of the family are no longer useful.

(20 marks)

It is a good idea to identify who the 'some sociologists' are. The item is suggesting the debate for you, so use this as the basis of your essay structure. Remember to bring in other relevant material from your own knowledge. You need to decide what argument you are going to make before you start writing your essay, so that your argument is clear.

Question 1: Student A

The decreasing fertility rate has led to smaller nuclear families. a As Sharpe found, women have become increasingly career-centred. In her research, using unstructured interviews in the 1970s and then again in the 1990s, Sharpe found that girls' aspirations had shifted from being married and having babies to having a career as the top priority. b This has led to women having babies later, meaning less time to have children as well as perhaps reduced fertility. It is very difficult to have a demanding career and many children, so women today are choosing to have fewer babies so that their family is more geographically mobile and manageable. c Stacey, a postmodernist feminist, sees this increased choice for women within contemporary global society as a very positive thing as women are not simply expected to have babies and stay at home. d However, this is not true of all women: for example, non-British-born women have a higher fertility rate (they have on average 2.3 babies), meaning that not all families are smaller. e

Furthermore, another way that declining fertility rates have led to changing family structures is that there are more childless couples. f One in four women now choose not to have children and are picking alternatives to the traditional nuclear family such as LAT, living apart together. g This means that people may be in a relationship but not living together. h As both partners now typically work and are more affluent, people may be able to afford two separate houses. In addition, globalisation has meant people need to be geographically mobile, as they are expected to work in different places. i There is much less stigma today about women not conforming to becoming a mother, and feminists such as Oakley argue that the nuclear family

a A clearly started paragraph, with a way clearly identified. The student sticks to their point, successfully developing it using relevant material. b Mentioning the methodology used in Sharpe's study is a good way to show analysis. c Nicely unpacked point: good analysis showing the effects of increased career-centredness, using sociological terms like 'geographical mobility'. d Going further: deeper analysis with Stacey, showing deeper and broader knowledge. e Good analysis here too, making clear the trend cannot be applied to all women.

f Clear second way, straight to the point. g A useful statistic and use of concepts. h The point is applied to the question and unpacked. i Globalisation identified as one reason for the increase in childlessness; good focus. j and k Drawing on other perspectives here, showing good sociological knowledge and understanding.
10/10 marks awarded.

can be oppressive for working women, with the dual burden (the strain placed on women through having childcare, housework and paid work) actually discouraging women from motherhood. 🅘 On the other hand, Beck argues that increased choice in family structures results in increasing risk and instability in family life. 🅚

Question 1: Student B

The fertility rate is the number of babies a woman has in her fertile years. 🅐 This has dropped considerably since 1900 for a wide range of reasons including contraception, fewer babies dying due to infectious diseases and women having careers. 🅑 This means that there are fewer children in society which leads to an ageing population. This leads to a range of problems including women having to take care of elderly relatives and their grandchildren. 🅒 Fewer babies being born means that the roles in the family are changing, with women going to work and men having to do more as a result. 🅓

There are more single-parent families in society nowadays. 🅔 Women can choose their own family structures, so some women are choosing to leave their husbands and raise their children on their own. This is more possible if there are fewer children. 🅕 Dennis and Erdos, who are New Right thinkers, argue that fatherless families lead to problems in society. 🅖

🅐 It is useful but not always necessary to put a definition of a rate in. This definition is not complete, however. Make sure you use accurate definitions. 🅑 The question is not asking about reasons for changes in the fertility rate, so this point lacks focus on the question. 🅒 The question is not asking about the consequences of changes in fertility rate for age distribution, so this point is at a tangent to the question. 🅓 A common mistake here: the student has talked about the impact on roles, not structures, of the family.

🅔 It is true that there are more single-parent families but there is not a clear link between this and decreasing fertility. 🅕 There is a notion of choice here, which is good, but still it is not linked to the specific question about structures. 🅖 Sociological knowledge, but not relevant to the question.
4/10 marks awarded.

Question 2: Student A

As suggested by the item, power relations refer to who has control in a relationship, and a way of this being measured is through decision making. 🅐 Edgel found in his research into decision making that relationships remain patriarchal, or male-dominated, because men continue to make the really important decisions in family life, for example about moving house and buying expensive items like cars. Women, he found, take decisions about less important issues such as what to eat or children's clothing. 🅑 This reveals that although more women earn more money recently, they still have less power in the family. Furthermore, 🅒 Pahl and Vogler found that the way couples manage their finances shows how relationships remain patriarchal. For example, they found that men still control most of the finances. They said, however, that things are becoming gradually more equal as there are more couples who 'pool' their finances, by having a shared bank account. 🅓

As suggested by the item, conflict in the family often leads to patriarchal patterns in relationships. Dobash and Dobash found in their classic research that one in four women experiences domestic violence. 🅔 This suggests relationships are very controlling and damaging for women. They used unstructured interviews to gain rapport with victims of domestic violence and found rich data: for example, on average women experience 28 incidents of domestic violence before reporting it to the police. 🅕

🅐 Good start, clear link to the item. 🅑 An appropriate study, well understood and explained, with examples. Excellent application to the specific question. 🅒 Analysis developed here, breaking down the issue by offering further evidence. 🅓 Interesting and relevant point which challenges the assumption that relationships are always unequal by noting that instead they may be changing.

🅔 Again, a well-identified hook from the item, using an appropriate and relevant study. 🅕 Good knowledge of the study including methodology. Could have developed the point further and applied it more successfully to the question. More analysis needed for a higher mark.
8/10 marks awarded.

Question 2: Student B

Oakley argues that women still do much more housework as well as paid work, so relationships are not equal. In fact, women feel like they suffer a 'dual burden'. This makes them feel powerless. [a] Dunscombe and Marsden found that women feel emotionally deserted. Although men might be doing more to help in some ways, they tend to pick the nice bits of family life, like taking the children for a nice day out. So, as in the item, there are a number of ways in which relationships are still not equal. [b]

As said in the item, men are often still in control when it comes to relationships. For example, Dunne found that when lesbian couples have a relationship there are no set of 'gender scripts' or ideas about what men and women should do traditionally. [c] In contrast, in relationships between men and women, there tend to be men controlling women, which we know because domestic violence is usually by men towards women. However, recently it has been shown that one in six men experience domestic violence too. [d]

[a] Housework isn't the focus of the question. It is not clear which hook is being used from the item. [b] There is some application, but unfortunately this is not relevant to the question. [c] A better start to the paragraph, but unfortunately Dunne's study is not relevant material to make the argument. [d] This point is better, as it focuses on the issue of power. It needed to be developed and analysed, however.

4/10 marks awarded.

Question 3: Student A

As the item suggests, a structural theory argues that the individual is shaped by these invisible social forces, and that the individual is passive in family life; examples are functionalism, Marxism and feminism. However, agency-based theories disagree, such as interpretivism, which claims that individuals can choose the kinds of family life they want and negotiate relationships. More recently, postmodernists argue that family life has moved beyond structure and agency, and today people act as individuals. [a]

Functionalists such as Parsons claim that the family is essential in performing two functions: primary socialisation of children and stabilisation of adult personalities. In other words, the structural forces are positive and benefit the individual and society. [b] Durkheim argues that we need structural forces in family life, as otherwise there will be anomie (normlessness) and then breakdown in society. Feminists are critical of this view of family life because they argue that structural forces are actually detrimental to women. [c]

There are different types of feminists, but they all agree that women are oppressed by patriarchal ideology — a set of ideas which means men are dominant in family life and society. [d] Radical feminists such as Millett argue that all ideas about the family need to be rethought, to remove patriarchy. Liberal feminists, on the other hand, believe that patriarchal structures can be improved, so that as society changes, attitudes and laws can reflect greater equality. For instance, they claim that women today can divorce men if they feel oppressed, and there is less stigma about divorce today. [e] Feminists argue that structural forces are therefore not very positive. This approach

[a] A good introduction which sets out the debate. This student knows what structural and agency-based theories are and recognises that postmodernism may today be more relevant. [b] The student is applying their knowledge well here to the question. [c] Good analysis and then evaluation of the functionalist view using feminist views, which link to the next paragraph. [d] Nice level of detail, recognising different approaches within feminism. [e] Good use of examples, to support the point made.

is really more useful than functionalism, because many women still experience domestic violence, and also 70% of all divorce is petitioned by women, suggesting that family life is not always easy for women.

Marxists claim, similarly, that structural forces shape family life to support the capitalist economy and values. 🔲 So, Zaretsky argues that the family acts as a 'buffer zone' where men's frustrations with capitalism can be taken out without challenging capitalism. Althusser says that the family is part of the ideological state apparatus, which means that people in the family are taught to believe that they love their family and that things are positive, so they accept their exploitation at work. In some ways this is a very useful structural approach as it shows how the family plays an important role in supporting the economy, by making sure men go to work and there is stability. 🔲 On the other hand, perhaps nowadays people have greater choice or agency than when Marxist ideas were developing. Society and family life have changed a lot. 🔲

Interpretivists argue that structural theories ignore the fact that family life is the product of negotiation and individual free will. Sociologists such as Allan and Crow argue that today people change family types over time, which they choose, so they have agency. Smart even argues that today people choose family members rather than accept the ones they are given by birth or marriage; she calls these people 'fictive kin'. This shows that in many ways, structural theories are no longer relevant. 🔲

Postmodernists go even further, arguing that we live in a poststructuralist world, so you could argue that structural theories are no longer useful. Postmodernist Stacey argues that this increased choice is a really good thing, especially for women who benefit most from being able to choose their family relationships. Postmodernist Beck argues that although there is a lot of choice today in the types of family life people have, this brings greater risk to family stability. This shows that today, perhaps structural theories are less useful because we live in a global, complex society where expectations about what we 'should do' are fewer and we think more as individuals. 🔲

In conclusion, structural theories such as feminism are incredibly useful for understanding family life. We know that women are still oppressed by the patriarchal family. But things are changing — perhaps now people have much more agency to choose family, and gender itself has become much more complex, with LGBT+ issues being more openly discussed. Maybe some of the ideas early sociological theories had are simply less relevant in a global, postmodern society. 🔲

🔲 Good evaluation; Marxism and feminist theories are both structural. The student might have said that they are also both conflict theories. 🔲 Good knowledge and understanding. 🔲 Good focus on the question.

🔲 A good counterview, well explained using analysis, with examples of relevant studies. 🔲 Developing the argument by exploring postmodernist views. Well explained. 🔲 A clear and strong conclusion, which fits the rest of the argument.

This answer is very clear, focused and accurate.
20/20 marks awarded.

Question 3: Student B

There are some theories that say that, as the item claims, people are shaped by structures. Others say family life is not like that and in fact people choose what they want. This essay will explore these issues. [a]

Durkheim argues that the family is really important as it maintains core values and makes sure that children are taught the norms and values of society. Parsons also argues that the family is important for stabilising adults. This shows that people need family structures to keep society working. [b]

Marxists argue that the family supports capitalism. It is important because it conditions people to accept that they are workers or the bourgeoisie. [c] Marxists like Engels argue that the family makes sure that wealth is passed down from one rich family generation to the next generation. Zaretsky says that the family acts as a buffer zone. [d]

Another structural theory, feminism, argues that women are oppressed by the family structure. Women have to put up with doing all the housework, for example. Oakley says that women have a 'dual burden' and Dunscombe and Marsden talk about women having a 'triple shift'. [e]

Other theories like the sociology of personal life argue that people can choose what they want to do in family life. There is no longer pressure to do what you should do — instead you can pick the family members you want. [f]

In conclusion, we live in a postmodern society today which is linked to globalisation. There are lots of different ways of shaping family life, so we act more as individuals. Therefore postmodernism is definitely the best theory for understanding family life. [g]

[a] It is not clear which views the student will explore, or that they understand what the difference is between structural and other theories. [b] It is not clear how functionalism is a structural theory, or if it is useful or not. [c] This is learnt knowledge which isn't being applied to the specific question. [d] This is relevant knowledge, but it is not applied to the question. It needs 'This shows that' to link it to the question. [e] Again, knowledge is not applied to the question. Concepts such as dual burden need explaining or unpacking. [f] Good counterview, but needs developing and analysis, for examples, studies and concepts. [g] The conclusion is not reached through discussion, and there is no mention of problems with structural theories.

This answer does not address the question explicitly and it is a little list-like. There is some relevant knowledge and understanding. It is not clear when the ideas emerged.
11/20 marks awarded.

Section B: Beliefs in society

Question 1

Outline and explain two reasons why some ethnic groups are more likely to be religious than others.

(10 marks)

> Remember ethnic groups are not all the same and there are very different patterns among different ethnic groups, so avoid making generalisations.

Question 2

Item A

In some parts of the world, such as South America, there have been times when people have turned to the church to try to make society fairer and more equal. In such cases, religion can be seen as a revolutionary force for change. In other cases, religion can cause significant shift in the economy.

Applying material from Item A, analyse two ways in which religion can 'act as a revolutionary force' for change.

(10 marks)

> For 'analyse' questions you need to choose two 'hooks' from the item. Base each paragraph on one of these hooks, considering carefully what you are going to say about each before you begin writing.

Question 3

Item B

Some sociologists argue that religion is in decline, because people today are more likely to believe in science and medicine, for example, to help them. Others argue that in postmodern society people are turning away from large, sweeping explanations altogether.

Other evidence points towards the view that rather than being in decline, religion is changing.

Applying material from Item B and your knowledge, evaluate the view that religion is no longer important as people today are turning to science.

(20 marks)

> This is a question which draws from a range of different areas of the topic. You will need to consider the reasons why science might appeal more today and evidence of secularisation, but also evidence and views which challenge the idea that people are less religious, in other words evidence of a resurgence in religion.

Question 1: Student A

One reason minority ethnic groups such as Muslims may be more religious is because, as Bruce says, they use religion as a form of cultural defence. This means that religion is used as a way to protect their religious identity in a culture which has a different set of beliefs. [a] Some suggest that this may be a response to negative views of Islam in the light of recent terrorist attacks by Islamic fundamentalists such as IS, for example the Manchester Arena bombing. [b] Cultural defence is perhaps a response, therefore, to Islamophobia. Bird suggests that Pentecostalist churches in the UK were a response to the traditional Christian Church of England not being welcoming to minority ethnic groups. [c]

Another reason why some ethnic groups are more religious is that religion can play an important role when someone moves into a country as an immigrant, as it helps them find community and support and friends. Bruce calls this cultural transition. [d] When people move into a new country, they need to make new ties and learn how to assimilate into their new home. The church provides a way to do this. Madood et al. found, however, that once the person has settled, the second or third generation are settled and so need less support from religious groups and are often less religious. Sikhs are a good example of this, as children of immigrants are less likely to practise their religion beyond the family. [e]

[a] Nice clear reason, concisely put. [b] Good use of a contemporary issue here. [c] Good analysis, using another example of how minority ethnic groups reached out to religion. [d] Another clear reason, set out clearly and separately from the previous reason. [e] Good analysis and evaluation, using another study and example. The candidate could have given just a little more detail on the Sikh example.
9/10 marks awarded.

Question 1: Student B

Some ethnic groups are more religious than others because they are more likely to have been brought up in a more religious family, so religious socialisation is more common. [a] Whereas white British children are often raised as non-religious, other groups tend to attend church more and be part of religious communities. [b]

Another reason why some ethnic groups are more religious is because they may be more marginalised, [c] which means that they are poorer or face discrimination on the basis of their ethnicity. They could turn to religion as a form of support and status in a hostile world that maybe is racist. [d]

[a] Although this a correct point, it is not directly answering the question about why some ethnic groups are more religious to begin with. [b] Again, this is describing how ethnic groups are more religious, not why. [c] This is a good reason for why some ethnic groups are more religious, and the student goes on to explain what 'marginalised' means. [d] This answer would have benefited from some studies and examples to develop analysis.
4/10 marks awarded.

Question 2: Student A

As the item suggests, in South America, there have been times when religion acted as a 'revolutionary force for change'. Maduro calls this 'liberation theology'. In South America, people turn to the church because there may be a corrupt government and nowhere else to turn for help. [a] So, people turned to their priests for help, for example, to tackle inequalities. Most people respected Catholic priests so in some cases, these priests were able to demand fairer distribution of wealth. However, this is often short-lived. [b] Another example of religion acting this way is in Burma where the monks led a peaceful protest in the streets to prevent human rights abuses and to challenge the unfair government. They helped create some positive changes, even though these were not long-lived. This shows how religion can act as a revolutionary force. [c]

In the item, it suggests that religion can cause a change in the economy. This was seen by Weber, who claimed that the change to

[a] Well-identified hook, referring to an appropriate sociologist. [b] This analysis shows good understanding. [c] Well-developed analysis using another example, Burmese monks. This is then applied to the question. [d] Another good hook identified from the item, concisely stated. [e] Excellent knowledge and understanding of Weber's study. Each concept is well unpacked. [f] Excellent application to the question.
10/10 marks awarded.

Calvinism from Catholicism in Germany, many years ago, led to huge changes in the economy. d Weber claimed that taking on the values of an ascetic lifestyle (not spending much, living frugally), seeing work as godly, or religious, and predestination (which made people anxious about God's decision to send them to heaven or hell) all led people to save money rather than spend it, which led to the emergence of capitalism. e Weber believed that this shows how small shifts in meanings in religion can lead to wider structural economic change. f

Question 2: Student B

Religion can cause social change, for example, in some parts of the world like in Germany. a Weber argued that being a Calvinist led to changes in society. Weber studied the way of life of Calvinists and said that their attitudes were very hardworking, and this meant lots of money accumulated leading to capitalist ideas. b However, some said that capitalism existed before Calvinism, in different parts of the world. c

In other parts of the world, religion has been used as a way of making a protest. d In America, for example, the civil rights movement leader Martin Luther King used religion as a way to stop racism. As the item says, religion can be really powerful as a revolutionary force. e

a The start of this paragraph could be made clearer, focusing more on the specific demands of the question, with use of the item. b Here it would have been good to bring in Weber's concepts, asceticism for example. c This is an evaluation point, which is not relevant to the question. It would have been better to develop the point further through analysis rather than add a 'bolted on' or learnt evaluation point. d Again, this paragraph would have benefited from starting with the item. e A good example, but this paragraph lacks sociological detail.
5/10 marks awarded.

Question 3: Student A

As suggested by the item, science has in many ways become more appealing than religion. Science can be defined as the belief in the objective method of studying the world, relying on empirical or observable data. Secularisation thesis sociologists argue that for a number of reasons, religion is no longer attractive today, particularly in a globalised world. Other sociologists such as postmodernists believe religion is changing but still important. a

Science emerged during the seventeenth to nineteenth centuries during the period of Enlightenment. People began to question the authority of the church. For example, Darwin's work on evolution showed people that humans probably evolved rather than being put on earth by God as his creation. b Science offered people solutions to problems like illness and it offered explanations for events like natural disasters. Unlike religion, science relies on rational, logical explanations which rely on empirical or observable data. The interpretivist Weber talks about how society has become rationalised. Unlike religion, science is an open belief system, so as Popper argues, it is based on the deductive method, where ideas are only acceptable until they are disproven. Recently, however, there have been doubts cast over scientific findings which may have been influenced by companies seeking to make a profit, for example Monsanto with its genetically modified crops, which has made people less trusting of science as 'objective' or value-free. c

a A good introduction, which sets out the shape of the argument and the main views, and uses the item. b Good understanding of science and a sense of when it emerged. Also good to use Darwin to explain how science challenged religious beliefs. c Good contemporary issue which supports the view that people are less trusting of science today.

As science has become more popular as a belief system, for example with the expansion of Western medicine, people especially in the UK have turned away from the traditional church. Today only 6% of the population attend church. Secularisation theorists argue that other indicators suggest people are less religious. For example, disengagement has happened. This means that the government has become more separate from the Church of England. For example, schools are less likely to use religious ceremonies. People are less likely to affiliate themselves to a religion, only 59% according to the 2011 census compared with 72% in the census before that. Also, people today are less likely to marry in a church or turn to the church in times of need. Bruce argues that the many recent cases of child abuse in the Catholic church have seriously damaged people's trust: for example, Cardinal Pell in Australia recently got imprisoned for child abuse. This suggests that religion is less significant as a belief system. d

However, some disagree and claim that rather than declining, religion is in fact simply changing. Davie, for example, argues that belief is becoming increasingly privatised — she says that today people are more likely to 'believe without belonging'. In a globalised world there is increased access to the internet and other ways of practising religion such as online, for example joining groups such as scientology online. Davie also says that many people practise 'vicarious religion' which means watching other people be religious without attending yourself, for example watching religious ceremonies on TV. This means that in some ways, there is a resurgence of religion, rather than secularisation. e

Postmodernists such as Bunting believe that today people are turning away from metanarratives like science and traditional religions and turning to more New Age movements and taking a 'pick and mix' approach. Some believe that religion is 'watering down' its own beliefs to be more appealing. However, this is not the case for everyone, as fundamentalist groups are growing, and people experiencing rapid social change may turn to religion for security and status. Bellah also argues that there is 'civil religion' today which includes things like worshipping the Royal Family rather than being traditionally religious. f The Kendal project asked, 'Has a spiritual revolution happened?' and found that although many people are no longer attending church in Kendal, in the UK, they are not turning to New Age spirituality instead — many of them are simply not attending religious activities at all. g

In conclusion, it would appear that science has been more appealing than the traditional religions. However, this does not mean that religion plays no role in people's lives. Rather, today people are more likely to turn to alternative religions and have a number of belief systems rather than place all their faith into one. h

d Good range of secularisation arguments, supported by sociological views and evidence. e Good evidence and arguments for resacralisation, drawing on postmodern arguments. f Good range of views on how religion is changing rather than declining. g The Kendal project is good here because it shows how although New Age spirituality is increasing, it is not increasing at a rate to replace traditional religion. h A strong and clear conclusion, which relates to the rest of the essay.
19/20 marks awarded.

Question 3: Student B

Secularisation theorists argue that religion is no longer important. Others say that science is important and has replaced religion. Today, science is where we turn for help with illnesses and disease, not the church. But there are some who argue that today we are still religious, as there has been the spread of ideas due to the internet and more travelling. [a]

Less people go to church than in the past. [b] We know that less people say that they are religious and there are fewer religious events at school. Children are less likely to be socialised into being religious. All of these things mean that people are less interested in being religious. This might be because people are growing more individualised, thinking of their own wishes and needs instead. However, Islam is growing fast, in the UK and in other parts of the world, so maybe it is just Christianity that is in decline. [c]

Science is generally more attractive to people as it helps them with illness and helps explain phenomena like AIDS. However, science has created lots of problems too, like global warming. Plus there have been examples of corruption, like drugs companies putting profit over safety. [d]

Today religion is still there but it is less formal, with young people for example seeing music festivals or being vegan as more religious than going to church. The church has lost its appeal to young people — Voas and Crockett call this the generational effect. [e]

Some people say that religion has become less 'authentic' and more 'watered down', meaning that religion has had to change and become more mainstream to appeal to people. There were and are problems with some religions not accepting same-sex marriage and this can put people off it as a belief system. [f]

Many people use New Age movements today, because they can use apps on their phone or get something from it that makes them feel more fulfilled. But these are really hard for sociologists to measure, so we do not know how many people are using them fully. [g]

All of these arguments show how religion today is in decline and science is more important to people. [h]

[a] A description of the belief systems but little evidence of the debate. It would have been a good idea to explicitly refer to the item. [b] Some evidence of secularisation here but lacks sociological detail, for example names, concepts and evidence. [c] An interesting point, but could have been applied better to the specific question. [d] Another good point, but is simply stated rather than linked back to the question. [e] The essay is becoming rather list-like at this point. [f] Some good points here; would have been better if the views had been attributed to sociologists or backed up with evidence. [g] Another interesting point, but again, not applied explicitly to the question. [h] This conclusion could have been developed, as this is a really complex debate. For example, the student might have mentioned that there are different patterns of belief systems within particular social groups and there is variation in different societies.

12/20 marks awarded.

Test paper 2

Section A: Families and households
Question 1

Outline and explain two ways in which globalisation has affected family structures. (10 marks)

Make sure you explain the effect of globalisation before linking it to the effects on family structures.

Question 2

Item A

Supporters of functionalism, one of the earliest sociological theories, argue that the family is beneficial to the individual and society. Some sociologists claim that this is not the case and even argue that family life reproduces inequalities. Others argue that the family unit described by functionalists is no longer the norm.

Applying material from Item A, analyse two problems with the functionalist view of the family. (10 marks)

Make sure you set out the functionalist view very briefly before you criticise it, using another perspective. Make sure your two criticisms are both separate perspectives and come from the item.

Question 3

Item B

The UK has one of the highest divorce rates in the world. There has been some debate about why this is the case, with some suggesting that changes in the role of women and a change in attitudes have led to this high rate.

Some sociologists see high divorce rates as a sign of higher expectations of relationships, while others see the high divorce rate as a social problem.

Applying material from Item B and your knowledge, evaluate the view that changes in divorce rates are a result of changes in laws and policies. (20 marks)

This is a debate about what is most likely to have led to the increase in divorce rates to the levels they are at today. Your task is to discuss a range of possible explanations for the divorce rate and then decide which reason is most important. You are also expected to consider whether the increased divorce rate is a good thing or not, from a range of sociological perspectives.

Question 1: Student A

Globalisation, which is the growing interconnectedness around the globe, has occurred because of increasing ease of transport. This has led to greater immigration, which has a number of effects on family structures. [a] For example, there has been a higher rate of immigration from within Europe. Often, a migrant will move from their country of origin and move to the UK to find work, and live in a shared household before moving their family to join them. High numbers of Polish families are nuclear and Catholic, and so have a lower divorce rate. This shapes patterns of family structures, as nuclear families are no longer the norm in the UK. [b]

Another effect of globalisation is that there is increased availability of methods of communication. People can chat for free online, and this makes it possible to have relationships over a long distance. [c] This has led to the increase in LAT partnerships, which means 'living apart together' where people are in a relationship but do not live together. Postmodernists such as Stacey would argue that this option is a product of the choices that globalisation offers, which are particularly beneficial for women, since it allows them to avoid traditional families which can be oppressive and patriarchal. On the other hand, Beck argues that such increased choice in family structures can lead to increased risk, higher divorce rates and so on. [d]

[a] Clearly identified way, well linked to the question. [b] This student really understands this example. [c] Another very clearly identified effect of globalisation on family structures. [d] Good use of theory here, as analysis.

Two ways well identified with some analysis.
8/10 marks awarded.

Question 1: Student B

There are more Indian families in the UK as a result of globalisation. [a] These are more likely to be extended than other families. This means that there are aunts and uncles or grandparents living in the same house. [b] This type of family is not very common in England. Brannen argues that this family type is good but that it can mean a lot of pressure put on children to do well in education. [c]

Globalisation has also led to more people from other cultures living in the UK so there are more single-parent families. [d] For example, African American families have higher rates of single-parent matrifocal families. This means female-headed families. [e]

[a] It would be good to say how globalisation led to more Indian families in the UK. [b] Good unpacking of extended families. [c] It is a good idea to use a study but make sure that it is focused on the family. [d] It would have been good to use the word 'migration' here. [e] Good use of a concept. It would have been a good idea to develop this, perhaps using New Right views on single-parent families.
5/10 marks awarded.

Question 2: Student A

As stated in the item, functionalists suggest that the family benefits the individual and society. Feminists argue that this is not always the case. Radical feminists such as Delphy and Leonard reject the functionalist view that the family is beneficial to women, arguing that actually women end up having to look after men and keep them happy, while men take the head of household position. [a] Dobash and Dobash go even further and claim that relationships are often abusive, with one in four women experiencing domestic violence. [b] This suggests that the family is not always beneficial, either to individual women who experience patriarchal oppression or beyond that, contributing to wider patriarchy in society. [c]

[a] A strong start, stating a functionalist view and then explaining the problem with it from another perspective, based on a hook from the item. [b] Good sociological knowledge to support the point made. [c] Good application to the question.

Another problem with functionalist theories, as suggested in the item, is that they presume that the nuclear family is the norm. In fact, today in the UK only 26% of all families are nuclear. So the assumptions made by functionalists about 'all' family types are no longer very useful. Rapoport and Rapoport argue that there are many types of diversity, including class, organisational, life stage and cultural variations. [d] Stacey, a postmodernist feminist, argues that in contemporary society there is much more freedom to choose the family structure you want, which is especially beneficial for women. Gernsheim argues that we have become much more individualist, thinking of our own needs in family relationships, rather than the assumption that we share values and ideas about the nuclear family being the norm. Therefore it is possible to argue that the functionalist view of the family is no longer useful today. [e]

[d] Another well-explained problem, clearly from the item. [e] Two postmodernist studies, appropriate for the question and well applied to the issue. Could have discussed another family type that has emerged as a result of the changes within society. **9/10 marks awarded.**

Question 2: Student B

Functionalists like Parsons argue that the family is positive and provides stability for adult personalities. He argues that also the family is a good place for children to be socialised. This means that they take a consensus view of society. [a] However, this may not be truthful because not everyone finds the family beneficial. For example, women may find it oppressive as they have to do all the housework and sometimes there is domestic violence in the family. [b]

On the other hand, some sociologists such as postmodernists argue that the family is not very similar to what it was. In fact, postmodernists now see the nuclear family as no longer the norm, as the item says. [c] Today there are many different types of families, for example single-parent families, families with no children, or those who simply choose to live on their own despite being in relationships. [d]

[a] It is not necessary to explain the view you are going to criticise using names or detail. [b] It would have been better to use another theory to build your criticism — feminism would have been good here. This paragraph lacks sociological names and concepts.

[c] The start of the paragraph could have been clearer and said in fewer words. [d] This is a correct point, taken from a hook in the item, but it is not developed with sociological concepts or studies. It also lacks application, for example 'this suggests that'.
4/10 marks awarded.

Question 3: Student A

As the item suggests, divorce rates in the UK are very high, with 49% of all marriages ending in legal termination. The divorce rate has been increasing steadily for 40 years, for a number of reasons including changes in divorce laws, a shift in attitudes and secularisation. Sociologists take a range of different views on the increase in divorce rates. [a]

Until 1969, there had to be a specific reason to divorce such as adultery or abuse. The 1969 Divorce Reform Act changed this because it made it possible to use 'irretrievable breakdown' as a reason for marriage to end. The divorce rate almost trebled. [b] The fact that 70% of divorces are petitioned by women suggests, as feminists argue, that marriage is very oppressive for women. Oakley, a feminist, argues that many women experience the 'dual burden', the strain of having to do housework and paid work, as an example of the patriarchal nature of family life. Liberal feminists see law changes as an improvement, arguing that gender equality is possible. [c]

[a] A good introduction, setting out the debate clearly and concisely. [b] A good explanation of the 1969 Divorce Reform Act. There could have been more divorce legislation included, however. [c] Good use of feminist theory and research here to analyse the reason for the increase in divorce.

On the other hand, feminists such as Sharpe argue that women are becoming increasingly career-centred and this makes it more possible for women to leave their husbands. Sharpe carried out research using unstructured interviews, in the 1970s and 1990s, on working-class girls in a London comprehensive school. She found that girls' aspirations changed from wanting to be housewives and mums in the 1970s to prioritising careers in the 1990s. This suggests that women are much more likely to be independent financially and as a result, can leave their husbands and support themselves and their children, which may explain the high divorce rate. d

Others cite a change in attitudes as the reason for the increased divorce rate: secularisation, the decline in religion, has led to less stigma surrounding divorce. As religion has less control over family life, people are increasingly cohabiting or choosing alternatives to traditional heterosexual marriage. The 2014 Same Sex Marriage Act was an example of this, and many marriages today take place in a non-religious setting. e Giddens argues that people today are much more interested in 'pure relationships', meaning emotionally satisfying relationships, rather than thinking about what we 'should' do. Stacey, a postmodern feminist, argues that this is a really good thing for women, who benefit from choice. Postmodernists in general argue that we are increasingly individualistic, for example Gernsheim. This would also help explain the high divorce rates. f

On the other hand, 80% of people who divorce now remarry, which suggests that people still like the idea of marriage, rather they are serial monogamists; individuals favour one long-term relationship after another, rather than seeing marriage as for life as people did before. The functionalist Fletcher sees increased divorce as a positive sign that people have higher expectations of their partner. However, not everyone sees the high divorce rate as a positive thing. New Right thinkers such as Dennis and Erdos argue that they result in fatherless families which lead to young boys having no male role model, which means they may be inadequately socialised. g

In conclusion, changing laws have definitely contributed most to making divorce easier and more accessible, although this cannot be separated from other social changes such as increasing acceptance of alternative ways of arranging relationships in a global postmodern society. Many see this as a positive, especially for women, who are most likely to see marriage as oppressive. It is worth noting that divorce rates are actually dropping slightly at the moment. h

d Another alternative reason suggested for the increase in divorce. Clear signs that the student is creating a debate. e Another good reason, with a contemporary policy introduced. f Another theory introduced here, postmodernism, to analyse the reason of secularisation/changing attitudes. g More theoretical views on divorce, both positive and negative — an excellent range of views in this essay. h A clear and decisive conclusion, with a good link to globalisation as well as recent trends. **18/20 marks awarded.**

Question 3: Student B

Divorce rates, which means the number of legal endings of relationships per year on average, have been going up steadily over the past 50 years. [a] Some sociologists see this as a positive thing because it means people are able to leave abusive relationships, but others see it as a real problem for society. [b]

In 1969 the Divorce Reform Act led to more divorces, because it was made easier and cheaper. [c] This meant many people who had been unhappy could decide to divorce. This led to changes, for example more single-parent families and more reconstituted families. Also there are more alternatives such as living apart together, so relationships are changing as are family structures.

Today there is less negative stigma of people who divorce so people are less worried about going through it. This means more divorces are happening in society. New Right thinkers say this is a real problem as it leads to single-parent families that have no male father figure and then the sons turn to crime. [d]

People are less religious today, so they don't see religion as a reason to stay together. A decline in religion is known as secularisation, which is definitely happening. [e] Postmodernists say that today, because of globalisation, people are thinking more about what they want, not what other people want.

Feminists think that divorce is good because marriage is often damaging to women because it is still patriarchal. [f]

Sharpe found that today women are more career-centred, which means they put their careers first before relationships or family. Girls are doing better in education which means that women now support themselves rather than having to depend on their husbands for financial support. So, this means that they can afford to divorce their husband and live on their own. [g]

[a] Incorrect definition: the divorce rate is the number of divorces per 1,000 married people per year. [b] Avoid saying 'some' sociologists — be more specific. [c] More detail would have been useful here about what the act introduced, i.e. irretrievable breakdown as an acceptable reason for divorce. [d] The essay becomes rather list-like here, with reasons for divorce listed without any debate about which reason is more or less significant. It would have been useful to state that it was Dennis and Erdos who claimed single-parent families lack male role models which can lead to issues with discipline among young boys. [e] It would have been a good idea to explain more clearly how secularisation has led to an increase in divorce. [f] More analysis or development of each theoretical perspective would have been good here. [g] This is a good point, but again, a little list-like, and the essay lacks a conclusion.

This essay fails to refer to the item explicitly.
13/20 marks awarded.

Section B: Beliefs in society

Question 1

Outline and explain two ways in which religion may reproduce patriarchal ideology. (10 marks)

Think about using two different ways in this question; avoid picking two reasons that might overlap. Make sure that you select and use examples that are not all from within Christianity; rather, draw examples from a range of religions to support your answer.

Question 2

Item A

Globalisation has sped up due to increased communication, for example through the internet and social media. Also, improved transport has resulted in increased migration. This has led to a number of effects on religiosity in the UK and beyond.

However, the effects of globalisation are varied, as it is happening at different rates in different parts of the world.

Applying material from Item A, analyse two ways in which religion has changed as a result of globalisation. (10 marks)

For 'analyse' questions you need to choose two 'hooks' from the item. Change can mean an increase in religion, or a decrease, or a change in the way that people practise their beliefs. Make sure you give good examples to support your points. Avoid simply describing a religion; make sure you link it to the question.

Question 3

Item B

Some sociologists see religion as playing a positive role for individuals and society, whereas Marxists see religion as reinforcing and maintaining inequalities in society. More recent sociologists point to the ways in which Marxist ideas are no longer useful for explaining the role of religion because the world has changed significantly since the time in which these ideas emerged.

Applying material from Item B and your knowledge, evaluate the view that Marxist perspectives are most useful for understanding the role of religion in society today. (20 marks)

Do not forget to discuss a range of views in this essay. Begin with Marxist ideas followed by neo-Marxist ideas and then go on to criticise these from a range of other perspectives. Avoid simply writing what you know about every theory: decide which you believe is most useful for understanding the role of religion today and develop your argument around that view. The conclusion should reflect your view.

Question 1: Student A

Religion can reproduce patriarchal ideology, or a set of ideas which support male dominance, in a number of ways. [a] The first is in the patriarchal hierarchies that exist in most religious organisations. Although it has recently become possible for women to be ordained as priests (and even more recently as bishops) in the Church of England, [b] most senior figures in religions are male. This is what Armstrong calls the 'stained glass ceiling', which means that women are effectively controlled by men in religion. In other religions this is the case too, although there have been female rabbis in Judaism for some time. [c] Feminists like Daly are critical of the patriarchal nature of traditional religions. El Sadaawi argues that Islam is actually quite gender equal, but that men have controlled the dominant positions in the hierarchies and have misinterpreted the Qur'an to their own advantage. [d]

Another way that religion can be seen as patriarchal is in the imagery used in religious texts. [e] Daly argues that Christianity has reinforced ideas of men being all-powerful and of course Jesus was a man and God is thought of as male. Daly argues that in the past, there were female goddesses, but these were not part of Christianity. Women in the Bible, for example, are seen as either 'pure and virgins' or else like Mary Magdalen, fallen women. Daly argues that such imagery sends powerful messages to women that they must try to be 'pure' and 'chaste'. [f] This means that religion acts as a form of social control, because to be a 'good' religious woman means to be docile, accept a husband's authority and take on traditional female roles. However, some argue that things are changing and that New Age movements offer women greater comfort and freedom from traditional views of women. [g]

[a] Good unpacking of the concept of patriarchal ideology. [b] Good contemporary evidence. [c] It is good that other religions are drawn on, rather than just using Christianity. [d] A good analysis of the way men have misinterpreted a religious text in their own favour. [e] Nice and clear; concise identification of a second way. [f] Good use of sociological knowledge here, very focused on the question. [g] Good evaluation and analysis, although an example of such a New Age movement would have been good.
9/10 marks awarded.

Question 1: Student B

Some religious buildings do not allow men and women to pray together. According to sociologists, this means that religion perpetuates patriarchal ideas. This sends the message that women are polluting and dangerous rather than equal to men. [a] Luckily today, not all women have to go to church. This pattern varies in different religions and in different countries, where some may be much stricter than others. [b]

Women are much more likely to be religious. This is because of the way that they are socialised into being more conformist, because of patriarchy. [c] They are made to wear veils and do what their husbands tell them. [d] But some women see the veil as a really good way to avoid being seen as sex objects. [e]

[a] A good start but it is not developed using examples, or by using sociologists' arguments. [b] It would have been good to give some examples from different religions and geographical locations. [c] Although this is correct, it is not answering the question. [d] This is a good point, but it is unfortunately not developed using sociological ideas, arguments and evidence. [e] A good point; could have used some empirical evidence to support this claim.
3/10 marks awarded.

Question 2: Student A

As suggested by the item, globalisation, the growing interconnectedness of the world, has been faster due to increases in forms of communication, such as the internet. The internet has led to the spread of ideas. This has led to the growth and spread of religious ideas and practices. [a] For example, many New Age movements can be accessed by using the internet, such as scientology. So where you live doesn't matter anymore — you can be part of a religion. Also people can access a range of religions through increasing numbers of online religious ceremonies. Davie says that religion is becoming more privatised and that people today believe without belonging, or turning up at their local church. This suggests that globalisation has led to a resurgence in religious and spiritual ideas. [b]

Another way that globalisation has affected religion is that it has led to greater migration, as transport has become much more effective and there is much more uncertainty and rapid social change. When people move into a new place, they need religion to help them settle into their new home, to find communities. [c] Bruce calls this cultural transition. People also feel like they need to defend their religious beliefs in the face of threats of change, which Bruce calls cultural defence. Unfortunately such rapid social change has also led to the growth of fundamentalism, or returning to a traditional interpretation of religious texts due to the fact that people are worried about liberal values removing traditional ideas: for example, Christian fundamentalist groups like Westboro Baptist Church which rejects homosexuality. All of these changes have led to religion changing and being used to respond to rapid social change and uncertainty. [d]

[a] A very clear start; well-explained effect of globalisation which is then linked to a change in religion. [b] A good example given, and good analysis through Davie's ideas. [c] Another appropriate hook used from the item, well explained and developed. [d] Well-developed analysis and example used that is appropriate and linked to the question.
10/10 marks awarded.

Question 2: Student B

The internet has led to a lot more opportunities for fundamentalist groups to spread their ideas. [a] For example, IS had 40,000 accounts on one social media platform. [b] This is not good because the social media providers should monitor how their sites are being used. IS use the internet to recruit members and spread their ideas. Also groups like Westboro Baptist Church use the internet to promote their controversial ideas, despite the fact that they want to go back to the past and have traditional lives. [c]

Being able to move more easily around the world means that more people are migrating. [d] High levels of migration can make people feel defensive about needing to protect their own religion, so some people are becoming very religious in response. For example, some young Muslims experience Islamophobia and so in response may become radicalised. Even women recently have been recruited to radical groups through the internet. [e]

[a] Good point, but needs to be linked to globalisation. [b] Excellent contemporary example, but needs to be applied to the question. [c] Good point, but could do with some sociological concepts, arguments or evidence in this paragraph. [d] The student does not link increased migration to globalisation or use the item explicitly. [e] A potentially relevant example, but not applied to the question.
4/10 marks awarded.

Question 3: Student A

As suggested by the item, there are a range of views on the role of religion in society today. Classical Marxists and neo-Marxists argue that religion generally reinforces capitalism, although neo-Marxists show how at times, religion can be used to challenge the system. Functionalists disagree with Marxists, arguing that instead of reproducing inequalities, religion actually creates greater social solidarity. However, postmodernists argue that the classical social theories are out of date and that it is better to try to understand the role by looking at patterns today. [a]

Classical Marxists claim that religion is a social construct, built by society to brainwash people into accepting capitalism without questioning it. Marx argued that religion was like a cushion to the oppression of capitalism, an 'opium of the people'. Lenin saw religion as being like 'spiritual gin'. Althusser saw religion as part of the ideological state apparatus, encouraging people to accept the system and love it rather than realise the true extent of exploitation. Hymns and religious texts, written by the ruling class, talk of heaven for those who work hard, so religion explains away inequality — it is a theodicy of disprivilege. However, neo-Marxists argue that at certain times and in certain places, religion can actually be used to challenge the unfair capitalist system. [b]

Maduro argues that religion in Latin America, for example, can be used as a way to challenge corrupt capitalist practices. He calls this 'liberation theology'. It was relatively short-lived, however. There are other examples of religion being used to challenge unfair capitalist systems, such as the Burmese monks challenging unfair practices. However, functionalists would challenge these views, seeing religion not as upholding inequalities, but rather as being a positive force, bringing people together. [c] For example, Durkheim talked of religion bringing people together to worship society. He uses totemism in Australia as an example of this use of religion for social solidarity and collective conscience. Meanwhile, Malinowski talked about how important religion is in terms of helping people cope with life crises and life events. So, rather than reproduce inequalities, functionalists see religion as a beneficial force in society. However, as we have seen in recent months, religion continues to be the cause of conflict all over the world, for example between Israel and Palestine, so functionalists' explanations may be considered overly optimistic. [d]

Feminists would agree with Marx — as conflict theorists, they too argue that religion reinforces inequalities and conflict between groups. However, they would argue that it is patriarchy that is being reproduced and legitimised through religion, not capitalism. [e] Daly points out how religious practices, texts and imagery all reinforce the idea that women are passive and powerless while men control and are all-powerful. El Sadaawi talks about the way that Islam is misinterpreted to maintain patriarchy for the benefit of men. So feminists would disagree with Marxist views but agree that religion furthers gender inequalities. [f]

[a] A good introduction, outlining the major views to be discussed and referring to the item. [b] Good knowledge of Marxist views, nicely linked to neo-Marxist views in the next paragraph. [c] Good use of functionalism here to evaluate. [d] Good use of a contemporary issue to show how functionalist explanations of the role of religion may be problematic. [e] It is a good idea to draw similarities between views, then draw out what is different, as has been done here. [f] This is good application and focus on the specific question.

By contrast, postmodernists believe that the world has changed and that traditional social theories are no longer useful for understanding the role of religion in society today. Rather they claim that religion in postmodern society is much more about fulfilling individual needs and is likely to be more commercialised and privatised, as people are less concerned with traditional values. Postmodernists like Lyon talk about the 'Disneyfication' of religious beliefs, a sort of watering down of religion, so it is made into an enjoyable experience. Bunting talks about how today people want to pick and mix various forms of New Age movements rather than turn to traditional religions. On the other hand, postmodernists also recognise how people may need religion more as there has been such rapid social change. Fundamentalist groups have grown in response to the 'clash of civilisations' as people seek to defend their religious beliefs and practices against what they see as the threat of liberal values such as gender equality or same-sex relationships. g

In conclusion, although classical social theories such as Marxism have been useful for our understanding of the role of religion in the past, today many people are no longer religious or are turning to new ways of being religious through New Age movements, so perhaps postmodernism is more useful in a contemporary context. Furthermore, although there are definitely still massive disparities in wealth, gender and ethnicity have become increasingly complex and important ways in which people express themselves. h

g Good explanation of postmodern ideas, and how these are more recent and therefore more appropriate. Good analysis with examples of postmodern thinkers and concepts. h A strong conclusion that summarises the argument throughout the essay that classical social theories may no longer be appropriate for understanding religion in contemporary global society. **18/20 marks awarded.**

Question 3: Student B

Marx, who is a conflict theorist, said that religion blinds people to the fact that they are being exploited. Marx said that the ruling class use religion to keep working-class people in their place, because people cannot challenge God. Hymns that say things like 'the rich man in his castle, the poor man at the gate, God loves them all' lull people into false class consciousness because people believe that they will go to heaven when they die. So religion keeps capitalism going. a

Durkheim, a functionalist, argues that religion is a very good thing because it makes people feel like they are part of a group. Totemism in Australia, according to Durkheim, is where people express what their group means to them and celebrate the group. Durkheim calls this social solidarity. b

Weber says that religion is about meanings and in Calvinist Germany people changed the way they believed in religion and this led to massive changes in society, unintentionally. So people began to see working hard as making them a good religious person, and this meant they saved money rather than spent it. This led to the spirit of capitalism. c

Feminists do not agree with Marxists because they see religion as damaging for women, and they argue that it reinforces the idea that men are in control. For example, wearing a veil in Islam means women are not

a A basic account of Marxist ideas. This could have been developed using other Marxists and then neo-Marxists. b Some knowledge of functionalist views, but they are not linked to the question. c This is a basic description of Weber's ideas without any application to the question. The essay is beginning to feel list-like.

able to express their identity. In France women are not allowed to wear a veil in public. This shows how religion can reinforce patriarchy. d

All of these ideas are out of date. Today in postmodern society many people are not religious as much because of secularisation, so the arguments of Marx are not very useful. In fact, there are new ways of being religious that Marxist ideas can't explain. We live in a global society where there are lots of ideas about religion all competing. e

d Veiling is a good example. However, feminism needs to be used to challenge Marxist views rather than simply juxtaposing it (placing it next to) another view. e A good point; however, the postmodernist view should have been developed in more detail.
10/20 marks awarded.

Knowledge check answers

1 Almost everywhere else, but primarily at school, in the media and among peer groups.

2 There is little evidence to suggest gender roles are based on biological differences, which means Parsons' claims are problematic. In addition, gender roles differ between societies, highlighting the fact that they are culturally defined.

3 The practice by which one can have only one legal spouse at a time.

4 A set of overarching explanations, for example a theory or science.

5 The role of the state should be minimal according to the New Right, and individuals should take responsibility for themselves.

6 Liberal feminists see family life as improving for women with the changes in laws and attitudes, slowly moving towards greater equality. Radical feminists argue that the family and society require massive changes in order for life to improve for women.

7 A forced marriage is one in which at least one of the parties has not given their free consent. An arranged marriage is one in which someone else — a family member or a specialist agent — has played a part in bringing the couple together.

8 Divorce laws have made divorce easier, attitudes have changed so that divorce has become more socially acceptable, and more women have begun working and so can leave a marriage and support themselves economically, which was less likely to have been possible in the past.

9 Reasons include: many people in this age group are recently divorced; lone parents whose children have moved away from home; more LATs — people 'living apart together'.

10 Gender roles are socially constructed as they vary over time and from place to place.

11 The march of progress view on relationships is that relationships adapt over time and improve, and that relationships are moving towards greater equality. Women may also have more confidence, if they are financially less dependent on men.

12 Women earning more may lead to women having more equality within the family as their views and decisions about their own income may be more influential.

13 Domestic violence may be under-reported as people may feel ashamed or embarrassed or fearful of further violence for raising it formally. A person experiencing domestic violence may not be able to leave the relationship so reporting it may make things worse. People may worry that the police will not take the issue seriously.

14 He based his research on portraits which were not representative of the experience of childhood among all social groups. The portraits might have been favourable or lacking in validity.

15 The idea that traditional quality time with parents is being replaced with technology, for example giving children a computer game to play with rather than reading to them or talking to them, leading to a poorer quality of childhood.

16 A society in which the child's needs are prioritised.

17 Birth rate refers to the number of live births per thousand of the total population in a given year. Fertility rate refers to the number of live births per thousand women of childbearing age in a given year — the childbearing period is taken to be ages 15–44.

18 Lower fertility rates; choice; the changing role of women, who are prioritising careers over having children.

19 A population in which the proportion of people in the older age groups is usually as high as or higher than that in the youngest groups.

20 The net migration rate, which is the difference between the number of immigrants and the number of emigrants throughout the year.

21 Increasing numbers of traditional nuclear families; an increase in the number of alternatives to the nuclear family such as extended families.

22 The hypothetico-deductive method, or experimental method.

23 Science challenges the idea of creationism; science challenges the idea that events such as natural disasters occur for religious reasons.

24 By allowing people a chance to grieve and receive support.

25 Over land rights, such as in Israel and Palestine.

26 Religion acts like a drug to numb people from the pain of their oppression.

27 People are sceptical of science and religion due to the problems emerging such as exploitation and corruption.

28 Women cannot be ordained as priests in the Roman Catholic Church.

29 The status quo is the situation that exists at the moment.

30 Social media are used to promote the interests of some fundamentalist groups; for example, Westboro Baptist Church uses social media such as websites.

31 Certain bishops have seats in the House of Lords.

32 An ideal type is a kind of model of something that draws out its essential characteristics, providing a kind of template against which possible real examples of the phenomenon can be measured.

33 'Charisma' refers to a quality held by powerful personalities that attracts other people to them. A charismatic leader can then attract followers by the strength of their personality. Most charismatic leaders of sects are male.

34 Most people are innately sociable beings and someone with weak external ties would be likely to welcome the sense of friendship and 'belonging' found in the movement.

35 They are available only to people who have internet connections. It is very difficult to obtain a representative sample. It is not possible to be sure who is completing the survey.

36 At least partly for demographic reasons — immigrant populations tend to have a younger age profile than the host population. For black people of African origin, there is a strong tradition of evangelical Christianity, so they may be less likely than white populations to be undergoing secularisation in the younger generations.

37 Cultural transition, cultural defence.

38 An atheist believes that there is no god or supernatural being. An agnostic is not sure and therefore has an open mind on the issue. Put simply, an atheist does not believe, while an agnostic does not know.

39 People may claim to be practising without actually attending regularly.

40 Some New Age groups may be so small and/or secretive that few people know of their existence. Many New Age groups have such a loose, informal structure that either there are no 'members' in the formal sense or no membership lists exist.

41 A system of belief which rejects ideas of the supernatural and accepts scientific ideas regarding the nature and origin of natural phenomena; does not believe in an afterlife, suggesting that we give our lives meaning by seeking happiness and helping others to do the same; and believes that ethical and moral decisions should be based on reason and a concern for humans and other living creatures.

42 In Europe, secularisation is thought to be demonstrated by the fall in religious attendance and in those professing religious beliefs, while in the USA, it is suggested that it is the churches themselves that have become more secular.

43 China is a communist society and communism rejects the idea of religion. While there are government-sanctioned religious groups in China, their activities are controlled and religious activities may take place only within registered centres of worship.

44 Their congregations are younger and may have values which are less traditional and more contemporary.

Index

Note: **bold** page numbers indicate key term definitions.

Index